1

Scriptures ®© NIV International Version

All images and artwork and mazes © Wayne Kerr
All song lyrics © Wayne Kerr Music Publishing (ASCAP)

ALL GOD MOMENTS ® by the Holy Spirit

Printed in the USA by BookMasters, Ashland, Oh.

HAVE
GOD
AND
GUITAR
WILL
TRAVEL
BY WAYNE KERR

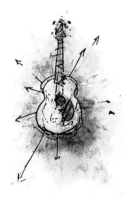

For Kelley, my wife and best friend. Thank you for being the woman of God that you are. You are the most amazing and inspiring person I have ever met. Thank you for always supporing me on all my crazy adventures. The best is yet to come. If anyone would like to read more about her, see Proverbs 31:10-31.

For my sweet parents, JoAnn and Roger Kerr, there is not enough room on these pages to say how much you mean to me, and all the ways in which you have supported me. Thank you for always telling me, "You can do whatever you want to with your life!"

My sister Terri, and bro-in-law Dave... for putting up with all the late night piano work down the hall from your room back in the day. Thank you for your hearts of ministry to others. To my New Mexico family, I never would have imagined that God would bless me in such a way as to allow me to be a part of such a fun and beautiful family. Thank you guys for all of your encouragement and love! I would not be able to stand without incredible family like you all holding me up. Thank you. I love you!

And to you reading this, I say thank you for the amazing opportunity to share what God has done and is doing in my life. I pray you will be encouarged in some small way.

# CHAPTERS

"The call on your life
will always be bigger
than you are."

- Pastor Randy Harvey

# CHICKEN AND SOME GANGSTAS

After 15 years of music ministry, traveling about 200 days per year and 8 CD's later, I decided I needed a retreat.

The summer of 2009 was insanely busy. I led worship for 11 weeks of summer camps in a row, and on the 12 week, did a 3 day "back-to-school" retreat. This was by far the most that I had crammed into a summer. Aside from those camps, I was booked for weekend concerts as well as leading worship on Sundays. Needless to say I was spiritually, emotionally and physically spent.

I've had a tradition of going away for a short retreat just before and after each summer. Before hand, to ask God to be glorified in the camps, to move in every single event that I am blessed to be a part of, and to ask God to literally give me the strength to make it through the schedule. After summer, it's a great time to refresh and thank God for His faithfulness, as well as wait for His voice on the next thing to work on.

My wife, Kelley, and I decided to take a road trip to New Mexico. Her sister had just had a baby. We combined our trip so we could see her family and I could sneak away to the mountains for a few days. Kelley's parents are retired in Ruidoso, NM. and it is beyond beautiful up there. For this trip we drove from Houston to New Mexico. We usually fly, but this time Kel and I opted to drive so I could bring my tent and camping gear in the back of my truck.

I left Kelley with her family, and headed out to go up the mountain. I've always felt it was important to go spend time alone with God. I figure if it was good enough for Moses and good enough for Jesus, it's good enough for me. Like many people, when I get out into nature, I am reminded of the bigness of God, my smallness, and the mystery of His desire to be deeply involved in our lives. His creation is truly something to behold. You know that feeling when you stand at the edge of the ocean or overlooking a valley. That feeling of, "Wow, there is a God, and I ain't Him."

My destination was a place called Monjeau lookout tower. It is within a protected forest area, and is manned by forest personal every day looking for forest fires. From up there you can see miles and miles in every direction. It is truly incredible. At 9300 feet elevation, even in late August, I needed a jacket. The drive from town up to Monjeau takes only 30 minutes or so, but part of that drive gets pretty intense. In fact, the road is closed off in winter months and is not accessible by car.

By the time I arrived that night, the sun was just starting to set in the mountains and it was already getting cold. I hadn't really thought things through, and had brought no firewood. I did have a small grill and charcoal to cook a few things, but nothing to create some serious warmth. I made the decision to go ahead and hang out til dark, cook some chicken, like a real mountain man, then head back down to the Kennedy's retirement cabin in Ruidoso. I figured I could get some firewood, blankets, and then come back up to camp the next night. I thought, "Since I'm up here already, and it's so beautiful, I'll hang for a few hours."

I turned off my truck and the sound of nothing-ness was overwhelming. There was literally no one up there! I heard a falcon off in the distance. I walked up on a few deer and I startled them more than they did me. The view was unreal.

I just sat there.

As my friend Winkie Pratney says, "When you come into His presence, you're dealing with the guy who created EVERYTHING."

The sun was beginning to set slowly, and the orange and pink sky was being painted before my eyes. It's funny how sometimes it takes a real moment of quiet before you can begin to truly deal with yourself. There were many changes happening in my music ministry that I had not chosen to deal with yet, but now this was the time.

Let me give you a little backdrop. In the past couple months several of my band guys, and best friends for that matter were needing to move on for various reasons. My man Raymond Turner, a drum king, keyboard stud, and producer extraordinare was needing to travel less and needed to step out. It was the first summer in many years without him there. Raymond has an amazing spirit, and anyone who knows him says the same thing, "That guy is one of the nicest and most humble people you will ever meet."

Shortly after, my good friend and talented guitarist, Matt Kidd - i.e. Frodo, as many of you know him informed me that he had a great opportunity to play with the Robbie Seay Band(Christian artist also based in Houston). Frodo played with me through the summer dates but then was needing to travel with Robbie. Throughout the summer I hadn't thought much about all these changes, mainly because I was super busy. But there I was with only that 1 deer, a few falcons, and miles and miles of expanse and silence.

I now had to deal with the issues at hand: My band as I knew it was no more. The band I had played with for the last 5 years had totally changed. Deep bonds are built between musicians who share music, worship, and travel together. It's almost an unknown language that is spoken between one another. Since more time is spent together off the stage than on, lasting and deep friendships are formed. I knew my friendships with both of these guys would continue, but the change was still something I had to deal with. I had a lot of questions for God.

Self doubt and lack of faith had been creeping in for weeks and I knew this trip was needed.

"What does all this mean?"

"What's next for me God?"

"Are my best days behind me?"

Even with years and years of seeing God's hand in my life, it only takes a split second to take one's eyes off of Christ. Just like Peter out on the water, as long as he was looking at Jesus he was cool. In fact, he was walking on water for pete's sake (pun).

Sometimes you have to fight. Fight through your own doubts. Fight back against the voices in your head that are negative. The enemy has been described in scripture as the liar and the deceiver. At best he can try to derail us from God's plan for our lives by whispering lies.

"Your best days are behind you."

"All that you did this summer was a waste of time."

"You'll never get another band together."

"You're too old to have any impact on these kids."

The devil would love nothing more than to take us down.

I started hearing the sounds of a few vehicles coming up the mountain. Within a few minutes 3 trucks drove past where I was setting up, each of the trucks had 3 or 4 guys in them. These guys didn't look too friendly, and I was glad when they drove on past me going further up the mountain.

At this point it was getting dark. So I was all about getting my little smokey grill going to cook some chicken! Even while setting up, I was prayerful, saying, "God what is happening in this situation?" "What is next for me?" "I feel discouraged."

By now it was completely dark and the only light was coming from the moon and stars and my small grill. The next thing I heard was the sound of one of those trucks coming back down the mountain. They pulled into the small clearing where I was parked and pulled into the single road entrance. The truck stopped. It was blocking the entrance and turned off it's lights then the engine. I thought, "Hmmm that's weird." I found it strange that with this entire empty mountain up here that they came into the area where I was, blocked the exit, and just sat there. No one got out of the truck and I couldn't see any movement at all. They were about 100 yards away.

At this point, I knew something was up. I tried to ignore them and go back to what I was doing. Then I began to pray, "Lord please protect me." About 10 minutes later another truck came down the hill and pulled up next to their buddies at the entrance. They exchanged some words then drove all the way up to where I was camping. They pulled up and parked right next to me. With an entire empty mountain all around, they came to park next to me?

I thought, "Ok great, here we go. I'm up here all alone and there's no one for miles and miles. This could be a problem." My brother-in-law told me to be sure and bring a gun up there with me, but I said, "Naaaaa.... I'm good." I heard the guys in the truck next to me yelling some craziness towards me, a lot of words that I won't type here. I prayed to God, and said, "Lord I know You go with me wherever I go and You are with me now and I know You will protect me."

I thought if it was one or two of them, I'd have a shot if things got iffy, but since there were like 8 guys... uhmmm .... God do your thing!

Here's where the story gets kinda funny. I put my stuff back into the back of my truck because everything in my spirit was saying to load up and get outa there.

I put my grill in the back of my truck while 2 pieces of chicken were grilling under the lid. I thought, "I'm not gonna let these guys get my food. I'm taking it with me!" I put my "still burning grill" into the back of my truck! I hopped into my truck and backed out of there. It was almost as if all those guys didn't see me. They had quit yelling in my direction, and were quiet. I feel like God was opening a path for me to drive out safely. The second truck backed out and cleared the entrance. I began to drive down the mountain. I know it sounds kinda strange to be reading this and fully understand what happened, just take it from me... I think God saved me from some mountain gangstas that night.

I drove the 25 minutes down to the cabin, with smoke rising from the back of my truck all the way down the mountain. I pulled into the drive, got out of my truck, and looked in the back. The smoke was still rising from my small grill. I took off the lid and the chicken was done to perfection! Best dinner ever. Pretty funny.

The next morning I was back up at Monjeau by the time the sun came up. These were the things I wrote in my journal during my time with Him up there that day. Maybe these things I heard from God were for me, maybe they might help you today:

"I am the vine, you are the branch. Abide in me, I will abide in you. With me you will bear fruit, without me you won't."

"There's stuff you still need to die to."

"Love Me, and then others."

"Your best days are before you, not behind you."

# THE PIANO ROOM

Where did all this begin?

I left Houston with my parents, Roger and JoAnn, in their small truck to be dropped off at college. I remember having a weird thought, "You know this will be the first time you'll have ever lived on your own." I was 19 and being escorted to my new life with pretty much all of my belongings in the back of a truck. Art supplies, clothes, no laptop since we didn't have those way back in the stone age of the late 80's, contact solution and a calling card. I was all set.

We arrived and unloaded at some dorm that looked and smelled pretty strange, and I was caught up in the moment of it all. *That's a fancy way of saying I was freaking out.* It wasn't until I saw them driving away that I realized, "Whoa this is for real!" I'm alone out here. Gulp. Shortly after my arrival I met Larry. Larry White, a cool guy who was trying pick-up lines out on an upper class girl. We hit it off and became friends. Later that year we became roomates, and are friends to this day. He even stood in my wedding as a groomsman. I was settling in. I had no clue the blessings that were in store for me during my time at college, no clue of the struggles either.

I was at school as an art major. Even as a kid I was always drawing and painting stuff. All through my younger years I was all about the art world. Even at the age of 12, I rented a booth at a comic book convention in Houston and tried to sell my drawings to people. I made $287 that weekend, pretty crazy huh?

The art building at school was a refuge for me. The smell of paint, turpentine, chalk, clay, and who knows what else was always in the air, I loved it. I shortly discovered that the art department and music department were connected by a series of buildings. I wandered down a hall that would set my life on another direction.

In the music building at school, there was a long hallway. Down each side of the hall there were 15 or 20 doors. Behind every door was a small room, 10x10 in size. In every single room was a piano. These were the practice rooms for all the music students at the school.

During this time, I became infatuated with the piano. I would mess around on the keyboard, not at all knowing what I was doing. For some reason I could hear a song on the radio and find the melody easily on the piano. I wasn't technically skilled at all, but it was amazing to me to press the keys, hear the notes, even feel the vibration of the chords working together.

Each day after class I'd walk over and find at least one room empty of an aspiring music student. I would just sit and play, not knowing what I was doing. Having no piano lessons in my life didn't bug me at all. Sometimes I got goofy looks from the music majors as they walked in carrying piles of Chopin and Bach sheet music, while I had my red backpack. Soon I was there every single day. It was a fun time, a good hideaway from the stress of class and social pressures, but little did I really know God was setting up a divine appointment with me.

One night early into my second year at school, I had an experience that changed me forever. I went over to find a room like usual to experiment with tone, melody, mood, and my overall lack of technical ability. The hall was pretty empty that night. I found an empty piano room and sat down. Closing the door behind me, I put my trusty backpack on the black, shiny upright piano and began to play.

The beautiful sounds of notes resounding together, apart, harmony, disharmony. I was getting lost in it. Then something changed. In a way that I can't really describe here, I felt the presence of God in that room with me. I just played and played and began to cry. As if through another pair of eyes I was seeing my life without Him. A life that was walking the fence. I believe that God spoke into my heart that night saying I was living 2 lives, and He wanted just one... mine.

For an hour or more, without pausing I played, cried, played, cried, and just poured myself out. God is so amazing in those times. When we are real with Him He cleans our hearts out like the most refreshing raging river. I felt the Lord revealing my messed up life to me, and my eyes were opened. And the crazy thing was, it wasnt judgemental, it was loving.

I remember that I came home that next weekend back to Houston and proudly told my mom and dad that I was ready to drop out of school and become a Christian musician! I'll leave that up to you to imagine how well that went over. I had just barely convinced my dad that I could even dream to attempt to make a living in the art world. He was slowly buying into that, when I came home with this revelation! Let's just say his response was, in it's edited version: "Get back on the bus... Wayne!!" We'll leave it at that.

Thank goodness my parents didn't allow me to even have a

second thought of quitting school. I did stay and get my degree in Visual Arts which I use still to this day. But the next couple years were full of amazing times exploring music. I wrote song after song. Most of which were really bad, but it was my honest heart. In fact, when I left school, I had a giant binder full of lyrics of songs, hundreds of them. My senior year some friends convinced me to enter a talent show and sing one of my songs. I was amazed to hear the crowd applaud, and was even more amazed when I won the event.

That night in the piano room would change the course of my life, and deep down I knew it. By no means did I walk out of there glowing like Moses off the mountain. It was just the beginning of a renewal in my life that is still taking place. Don't misunderstand me at all, I'm not a guy who has everything in the world figured out. I am a work in progress just like everyone else, leaning on Christ, and very in need of a Savior.

I believe that the process itself is what Christ loves to take us through, so that He can receive glory not only in the big moments of our lives but in the day to day stuff too. That night for me began the momentum in my life that is still spinning today like crazy. These pages will to the best of my memory, capture just one guy's journey. One in which an Awesome God keeps letting little tiny rays of His light be seen every now and again.

These pages are not the gospel according to Wayne, but they are a record of a bunch of cool God moments that I've seen. There area a lot of silly and fun moments here too, that's for sure. I hope you enjoy reading through these crazy moments, and I pray you are encouraged to trust Him and honor Him.

Oh and by the way, this adventure is not just for me, your piano room awaits too.

# FROM ART TO MUSIC

After graduating from college, I had the yearning in my heart more than ever to pursue music ministry. After graduation I had bounced around between a few graphic design jobs, but I was growing increasingly unhappy with it all.

I was working at Fiesta, a Texas-based grocery chain. No, I wasn't bagging groceries, I was working in the art department of their corporate office. The thing about the grocery world and advertising, they don't really put much emphasis on being overly artsy or creative. Everything revolves around the price! Basically once buyers get a good price on something, they would rush that to the the art guy (me) and I kicked out an ad really quickly.

For example, at the time (1995) I was in charge of the Saturday full page ad for the Houston Chronicle newspaper. Each week that ad cost the company $12,000. Can you imagine? And the amazing thing was, I would be waiting right til the deadline, and a buyer would rush in and say "Diet Cokes 12 pack for $1.99!" I would rush and throw the ad together, and out the door it would go. It wasn't exactly revealing the most artistic side of my abilities. Don't get me wrong, I was thankful for a job, but at the end of the day, I was realizing this wasn't the reason I was on the planet.

Also, DO NOT price something wrong. On my first day at the

job, they informed me that the guy I was replacing ran a soda ad for the wrong price. They said the company lost $60,000 over a weekend because the guy ran the price at 99¢ a 24 pack, not a 12 pack. EEEEeeep.

About a year into my job at Fiesta, I was trying to play music at any and every opportunity I could get around Houston. Any church youth group that would let me come in and share, I'd go. Then I got a chance to do a full week of camp at Lakeview Methodist Camp one summer. It would be my first chance to be there for an entire week. I took my 1 week of vacation, and headed off to camp.

I remember that the week was so incredible. All week was spent hanging out with kids, swimming, playing volleyball, eating bad starchy camp food, just overall crazy camp mayhem. But more importantly, every worship session was unreal and so powerful. There was a speaker there as well and it seemed as if all the talks were directed at me, not even the kids. It was truly amazing.

On the final day of camp, it was clear the bond that had been made with all the students there. Kids were all saying goodbye, exchanging phone numbers and addresses... (yes, real addresses-this was kinda before email addresses.)

I drove home so full in my heart and spirit. Tired beyond description, but so overjoyed. And on top of that, I got payed to be there!

I remember so vividly the monday morning after that camp. I put on my tie and dress pants, drove to work, and sat at my little desk in my little cubicle. I realized at that very second, that this job was no longer for me. To invest in people through music was life giving, and to be involved with music ministry was something I knew God was calling me to.

Over the next few months I continued to lay it at the feet of the Lord, and ask for His direction. I was ready to go and do it! But no doors seemed to be opening up. Have you ever been at a place like that in life? You seem ready for something to happen, and it doesn't. It can be pretty frustrating. With no idea what it would even look like, or what it was I was getting myself into, I just knew if it could be like that camp, I was in.

Several months later, still nothing opening up, I remember taking a long walk to have it out with God! I was living with my sister at the time, and there was a small park only a few blocks away. I headed there on foot, overwhelmed with a feeling of frustration. I knew that God had clearly given me this music thing pretty much out of nowhere. What I didn't know is why I now had this crazy desire to pursue music and ministry, and nothing at all seemed to be happening.

I walked through the park, talking out loud to the God of the universe. I cried out for Him to be present. I laid it all out there. I said that I didn't really know what was going on, that I had loved art my whole life, but now music and ministry had collided with that life path.

"God if this is You doing this music thing in my heart, I ask you to open the doors for me to be able to pursue it! If it's NOT You, then please God take this burden away. I'll strive to be the best graphic designer I can be, and I'll pray it will bring you Glory. Either way, I just lay this at your feet, it's making me crazy, and I'm not sure what to do. I will just rest in You!"

It's pretty amazing that even through the course of prayer, a person can feel their burden lift by just talking with Him. By the end of my hour or so out there, I found myself looking up the tall pine trees, enjoying the beauty of His creation. I felt at peace for giving the situation over to Him.

Literally that same week, I received a phone call from Nate Templeton. He said he got my number from one of the youth ministers that spoke highly of my music ministry. Nate began to tell me about an event that he was working with called "MidWinter" in the United Methodist Church. He said it was a series of weekends where kids get together from all over Texas and do a retreat. He asked if I might want to get involved! "Sure," I said. "Sounds awesome!" I tried to sound relaxed.

I remember so clearly the next thing he said. To this day I know, this phone conversation changed the course of my life.

He said, "We do 6 weekends spread out over January and February some Jr. high and some Sr. high weekends. Are you interested?" I looked at my calendar, which was COMPLETELY blank... and said, "I may have some free time, which weekend were you looking at?"

"What would keep you from doing all 6 weekends?" He asked.

I sat there in silence for a minute. "You there?" He asked.

"Uhmm yea, yes I'm here. I... I don't think anything would keep me from doing all the weekends."

At that moment, I felt the gentle touch of God reminding me that He was directly involved in my life. I thought of the day walking around in the park, when I laid this down at His feet. God was revealing Himself to me, and His plan too.

I did lead worship and sang some of my original tunes at all 6 of those weekends. At each MidWinter, there were youth groups from all over. Some weekends had 300 kids, some had 600... it was a big deal! After those weekends I was asked to come to youth group nights, camps, retreats, etc., and this began the next year and a half of working in design on weekdays and music ministry on weekends.

During those several weeks I had several confirmations of God's hand in my life. I also had a clear vision where I almost audibly heard God say, "I want to give you the desires of your heart. And for you right now, music is the desire of your heart. This will be the icing on the cake. The cake though... is ME."

I felt as if God was saying to remember now as life goes along to not only look at the blessing, but to look to the One who gives the blessing. Look not only to the hand that provides, look at the heart of the One who is providing.

Less than a year later, I had left my "day job" at Fiesta, and had stepped out in faith to pursue music ministry. I didn't know what that really meant, I just knew God was at work, and there was no way I couldn't respond!

Even as I start out typing these stories, I'm not even sure exactly why I'm doing it. I'll be honest. In some ways, I feel that it's crazy for me to write a book. Who am I? I will say that I feel so clearly God is leading me to put these stories down. They are in no particular order and they are only part of the bigger picture. These are the stories and moments that have come to my mind over the last 8 months of putting this book together. I pray you will go on this little journey with me. There are some hilarious (in my mom's opinion) pages awaiting you, and some that may challenge you.

"For I know the plans I have for you, declares the Lord. Plans to prosper you and not to harm you, plans to give you a hope and a future." Jer. 29:11

God has been beyond faithful to me.

He will be beyond faithful to you too.

MUSIC MINISTRY STORIES

PART 1

# BEARCAT BASKETBALL

When you go out into full-time ministry, you immediately start making wise choices right? I still had a lot to learn and a lot of maturing to do. In my early years of ministry, I was invited to lead worship for this youth leader's training weekend at Lon Morris College here in Tx. My good friend and soon to be parter in crime Micah Nicolaus was there speaking. This guy is hilarious. He is an amazing communicator who loves people, and he is an avid sports fan. I mean, this guy saw a game in every single Major League Baseball stadium in the USA in the same year... that's a sports fan!

One day we were having lunch with some of the younger youth pastor guys who were there. The conversation somehow slipped from ministry, to what sports teams we liked, to finally how old Micah and I were and how we could never hang on the basketball court. Our pride was at stake, and these 3 youth pastors all in their early twenties must have been on crack, so we set up the contest for that day at 2pm. 3 on 3. Young guys vs. the old guys. (We added a guy to our team that was also a bit younger to help us out).

A little before 2pm we headed towards the gym. When any athlete, or in our case, "former athlete" walks into an empty gymnasium or stadium, there's no way to suppress all of those feelings from long ago. Even though the facility was completely empty, in my mind I could hear thousands of screaming fans chanting... "old guys," "old guys," "OLD GUYS!!!!!"

Now I say what followed was Micah's idea, and he says it was my idea, but either way, this is what happened. The lure of the locker room called our names. As we entered the vacant locker room, we saw there before us, almost divinely placed,  glowing as if illuminated from the heavens: a large rack of Lon Morris Bearcats basketball uniforms.

Within moments the three of us ran out of the locker room onto the court, all dressed in our green and white uniforms. We were hyped.  As we ran single file around the court, our opponents who were now warming up, looked at us like we were crazy. We did 2 full laps before we started our pre-game lay-ups. Micah began the play by play, announcing the starting positions for this season..."BeeeeaaaaarrrrrrrrrrrCAT Basketball!!!!" I think if memory serves, he also turned on the PA system and used the mic at the scorers table to announce it there as well.

Now this was many years ago, and I have hopefully gained maybe a little more wisdom since then.  I do not suggest anyone use any equipment that they are not authorized to use. - *Disclaimer included at request of my wife.*

Back to the story.  Now honestly, today I don't recall if we won, lost or who made how many points, etc.  What I do remember is having a blast, and when the game was over, we went back to the locker room, and tossed our now extremely sweaty uniforms in a pile on the ground.

The next morning we heard a knock on our dorm room door. We opened it to see a fairly unhappy face of the man directing the event that weekend.

"Did you guys go into the gym and wear the basketball teams brand new uniforms to play around in? And then leave them in a messy pile on the floor? The team hasn't even gotten to wear them yet. I just got chewed out by the coach."

"Uhhmmm...."

Micah and I looked at each other....    "Possibly.    Yes."

# PITTSBURGH

A few years ago I was booked to play in the New York area. I was excited because it's not often that I got up in that part of the country. A friend of mine who is now in youth ministry in the Pittsburgh area saw that I was playing near him, and contacted me about stopping on my way to play for youth group.

We had figured out that my connecting flight was through Pittsburgh, and since the flight had already been purchased he offered to fly me home after the event. The plan was for me to buy another ticket home, and just hop off of my connecting flight and do an event with his kids.

The weather was cold. I mean I'm talking "I'm from Texas and ain't used to this stuff" kinda cold. I packed up what wintery clothes I had and headed out on my venture.

As the weekend in NY came to an end I made my way to the airport for my flight to Pittsburgh. I checked in at the desk, presented my ticket to Pittsburgh then onto Houston, but expressed to the lady behind the kiosk that I needed to check my guitar and bags only to Pittsburgh. I explained that I wouldn't be using the entire flight. Even in that pre 9-11 world, they wouldn't let me do this (to my surprise).

"If your ticket says NY to HOUSTON, your baggage has to go all the way to TX. You can't pull your bags off half-way. We can't stop you from getting off your connecting flight, but your bags are going to Houston if you get on this plane."

Yikes.

"Hurry sir, we are boarding now." She said.

"Uh-oh," I thought. A real delimma began to unfold before me. Really there were only 2 options here.

1) I get off the plane at my connection in Pittsburgh, and go to my friend's event... in this case I'd have no guitar to play, no cd's to sell, and in fact no clothes bag! I looked in the window reflection of myself, having not shaved, wearing my old school glasses, and sporting my uber-cool 90's slicky workout pants. Yikes. Not exactly my favorite look for a concert.

2) The other option was to call my friend to cancel, and say it just wouldn't work out this time. It's kind of hard to do an event with no guitar.

Option #1 also presented the problem of my bags and guitar arriving in Houston without me. I could just see them in my mind going round and round the baggage claim, and some guy saying, "Hey nice guitar." Get my point? I wrestled in my brain about what to do. I basically had 3 minutes to make up my mind. This was not only a convenience thing, but a spiritual decision that needed to be made. Was I willing to cancel a committment due to this inconvenience?

I called THE spiritual giant in my family, my sister Terri! She is an amazing woman of God and I think she honestly has a hot-line phone right to Jesus. Maybe more like a bat-phone, you know the old-school red phone from the TV show with only one button on it? Oh yea, I forgot... some of you probably weren't alive in the 70s. I explained the situation to her, told her what was up, and without hesitation she said "You have to go to this event".

"Honor your word, and God will honor that. Don't worry about your stuff arriving in Houston, it'll be ok, and we'll pray that it all stays safe!" She concluded our conversation the way she always does, "You're anointed buddy!"

Did I mention I have an amazing sister?

I felt a peace about it too.

Off I went. Me in one direction... to Pittsburgh. My guitar, pedal board, clothes, contacts for my eyeballs, cd's and shirts, all went back to Tx. Yay.

I arrived at the Pittsburgh airport, walked down the tarmac just in time to see a few folks standing there with a sign, "Wayne Kerr!!" I waved and walked towards them. Their facial expressions were priceless. Their faces said everything from "Really?" to "Surely that's not him" to "No one wears slicky pants anymore."

"I thought you'd have a guitar and a bunch of equipment," one of them said.

"You look a little different than in your promo pictures," said another one.

I explained the craziness of the morning, and we were off to the church. They said they didn't at all know what to expect as far as turn out, but that they had done all they could to get the word out. "Hey, we'll have fun whoever is there." I said.

That night I'd say that maybe 30 kids showed up in a room that seats about 800. Thirty isn't a bad number of kids to have at your youth group, maybe you just don't meet in a gi-normous room. I borrowed a guitar for the night, polished up my blue slicky pants (yep they were bright blue... didn't I mention that?) and gave it all I had.

I'd say at best the response was fair to less than average. I think 1/2 the kids were just distracted by how goofy I was dressed. I sang my songs, sang about my Saviour, shared about His amazing love. When it was over, kids left, and it almost seemed like a non-event to many of them. Then the youth guy informed me that I was welcome to sleep on the couch of his house or the couch in the smaller youth room, I could have my pick!

Yikes again.

He said they had no budget for a hotel room. "No prob," I said.

So that night I laid on an old couch in a church in the dark wondering what in the world I was doing in Pittsburgh, Pa. As I was lying there, I could see out the window into the very industrial and crowded streets of the city.

The next morning they dropped me off at the airport to head home, with a slightly stiff neck from the couch, wearing the exact same clothes still. I don't remember the flight home, I must've slept right through it. I arrived in Houston and went to the baggage retrieval area. My guitar, product and everything else was right there waiting for me. "Whew," I remember thinking as I drove home... "Man, was this even worth it?"

Fast forward now about 3 weeks. I was checking some emails and received one from a student in Pittsburgh.

"I just wanted to write you a note and say thanks for coming, and to let you know about a student up here in our youth group. She's going through a lot of problems. She had heard there was some guy from Texas coming to church that night to perform a concert, so she went ahead and came." The student continued, "I wanted to let you know that she did come, and heard your songs and your message. She has been through a lot, and has even been cutting recently, feeling as if she was at the end, with no hope. I wanted to let you know that she was touched that night, and that she felt God's love in a way she never had before. The girl is now plugged into the youth group again. I wanted to write you and thank you, because that girl... was me."

I sat in front of my computer, speechless, tears rolling down my face.

I thought about my selfishness. I thought how there was a divine appointment set up between this young lady, and God Himself. I thought of how I almost backed out of that because of a small inconvenience to me! Woe to me if I hadn't gone that day. Woe to me for all the times in which I HAVE sought my own will and missed God's plan for me, a plan that might have been not only for me, but that may have impacted other people.

That day I asked God to forgive me of my "me" mentality. He's still working on me in that area. I could almost hear God sarcastically saying, "Oh yea, I wanted you to go all the way to

Pittsburgh, Pa. so those kids could have a life changing encounter with YOU Wayne." No.

We go when He says go, when He says when. Not that anyone should encounter us, or be blessed by us, but that others may in fact have an encounter with HIM. I just encourage you today, while you read this, if you ever have even the smallest prompting of the voice in you which is the Holy Spirit obey it, right then! If God says, "Leave that girl a $20 tip because she is clearly struggling." Do it. If God says, "Say hi to that kid at school that no one talks to." Do it. If God says, "Go in my name to all the earth and proclaim my gospel, even if you're wearing blue slicky pants." Do it!

Go.

# WHAT ARE YOU ROOTED IN?

If there is one major drawback to this calling of full-time traveling music ministry, it is that I'm often out of town on Sunday mornings. Our home church is Grace Fellowship in Katy, Tx., it's pretty much amazing. Jim Leggett is an anointed teacher, and amazing Pastor, and I'm always blessed by his messages. Much of the time, even if Im traveling, I will download his messages online and check them out.

Last year, I was thankful to actually be at home for a few weekends, and found myself at Grace. One morning in particular, my brain was a little distracted. (I'm sure this never happens to anyone else out there during church) I found myself doodling on this prayer request card. Some of you may have heard me tell this story at one of my concerts. I began to draw a tree. You can see the actual scan of it here.

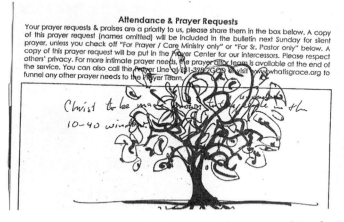

As I was drawing this tree, I almost felt the voice of God saying, "This is you Wayne, you're very busy. You've got all this stuff going on, and you are all over the place like these branches." As I continued to draw, I kinda started feeling full of myself, and my thoughts were like, "Yep that's me, I'm traveling all across the country doing shows. God even opened doors for me to play in other countries!" Then I drew the horizon line and added the roots.

I feel as if God then directed my attention to the roots in the drawing, as if He was saying, "This is the condition of your heart right now." My slowly growing sense of self began to shrink into an honest look at my "out of whack" heart condition. "Look at those little roots," I thought to myself. One little wind storm could come along, and that tree is done for.

Without really realizing it, I'd let my business begin to take the place of my relationship with the King. Yes, even in ministry with the best of intentions, anyone can look up and they are running off of the fumes of a once burning on-fire relationship with God.

Almost as clear as day, I could hear the Lord saying, "Turn that drawing upside down, that's the tree I would much rather see." As I rotated the picture around, I could see what He meant. I needed a much deeper root system, one that is strong. Then clearly that tree would grow even larger than the other one, healthier, and in fact be able to grow into what it was intended to become.

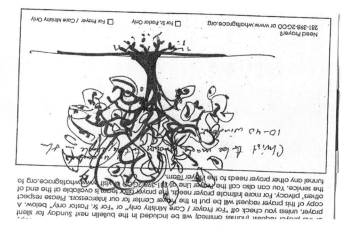

The bible says in the very first book of Psalms that God desires for us to be like trees that are planted by the river. A tree like that continually draws its nutrients day and night from the living source, good clean water.

My wife and I own 22 acres of land near Schulenburg, Texas where we go hang out, refresh, and spend time with God. There is no house, no power, no water, no toilet, just God's amazing creation. There is a cool rock bed creek that runs all year at the back part of the property, and it is totally lined with trees. You can see exactly what God is talking about when you walk around back there. Huge sycamore trees that tower high in the air have been drawing from this source for longer than I've been alive. Their golden and green leaves are not only so beautiful I can't describe it here properly, they also create one of the loudest natural celebrations when the wind goes through them.

One massive pecan tree has to be hundreds of years old. It is rooted by the river and drinks from it. You wouldn't believe pecan trees could get this big around!

Scripture says we are to be like a tree planted by the river. This tree will grow and become what it was intended to be, and most likely become more than it thought it ever would. God says the tree will not only bear fruit, but it will provide shade to the area, and even birds and other animals will take refuge there.

What are you rooted in today?

Are you someone who is like me? Without even noticing maybe we have gotten busy, maybe we have concerned ourselves more on how the tree looks to everyone else, and have not worried about the character, the root system.

The sap somehow mysteriously goes up and down the tree bringing life to it. The things you and I are rooted in will affect us deeply. TV. Facebook. Movies. Music. Friends. Career. Self. Popularity. Money. These things aren't necssarily bad, I just need to make sure that I am rooted in Jesus Christ above all else.

Draw up his nutrients today. Peace, forgiveness, purpose, joy, hope, real life. Not only will you grow into exactly what you were created to become, you might even have a life on your hands that is more amazing than you ever even dreamed.

*PS- My apologies to Pastor Jim for drawing in church instead of listening. I'm sure I downloaded your message the next week!*

# METRO BIBLE STUDY

When I first got out of college, my days of going to the piano room were over. I found myself back in Houston, looking for work in the graphic design field. When I was at home there was one GLARING reality that silently screamed at me every single day: I now had access to NO piano. Ugh.

While working to save money for my first keyboard, I would look for any opportunity to play on any piano I could find. We lived in the Heights area of Houston, and one of the churches near me was Houston's First Baptist. It's a great church, and at the time I began attending the newly launched Metro Bible Study for singles and college students.

I would often find myself up at the church even when no one

was around. The main auditorium is pretty huge there, I'm not sure, I think it seats 4000-5000 folks. Many days I would enter the large worship center and marvel at its size and how quiet it was in there.

One day the draw of the grand piano on the stage was too much for me to deny. I walked up on the empty stage and began to play on the piano softly. The natural reverb of the space was amazing, and when I looked up hours had gone by. I was lost in the music and the new desire God had planted in my heart.

Then I got escorted out by security.

Now that I look back, it is silly that I'd assume they would just let some kid walk in and play on the stage. I'm not sure what I was thinking. I would have kicked me out too!

It was pretty amazing less than 4 years later to be hired to lead worship at Metro. I was hired to walk onto that very same stage, sit at that very piano, and lead nearly 2000 people in worship. God was granting the desires of my heart.

God has a sweet way of reminding me not to despise small beginnings.

Never shoot down your own dreams, or let the small arrows of other's negative words deflate you in any way.

Dream even if it seems impossible. Say thank you when the creator gives you the desires of your heart.

# SEVENTY FIVE DOLLARS

I left my day job at Fiesta on May 5, 1995. Cinco de Mayo... the Mexican day of freedom! After a year and a half of doing music on the side, part time, it was time to take the plunge and go for it in a full-time capacity. I left my job in faith, and I knew in my heart God was leading me. I also had little to no cash, which leads me to this story!

My amazing sister and her awesome husband were gracious enough to let me move in with them right after I decided to go full-time with music. What was supposed to be only for a few weeks or months actually turned into about 2 years. I think I'll owe Dave for the rest of my life actually! They have helped me in SO MANY ways.

During this time I was starting to get plugged into a few local chapel services at area Christian schools. My great friend Robin Muller was helping me and a local DJ, Jeff Scott, from Lightforce 89.3 KSBJ FM Houston's Christian radio station. Robin was doing an amazing job at helping Jeff and I get into some schools. Jeff would speak and share his testimony, and I would do a few tunes, it was a blast. Sometimes we would do one chapel a week, even two. Many times we never knew what we were going to be paid, if anything, but it was usually in the $75 range each for coming out. This was a lot of money to me at the time, I mean A LOT.

I remember this one morning I headed out to do a Wednesday morning chapel event. I met Robin there at the school, and she informed me that Jeff probably couldn't make it that morning because he was sick like a dog. The principal said, "Wayne can you cover the entire chapel? Maybe you could speak and share your heart with the kids along with some of your music?"

"Great!" I answered. "No problem!"

Things went well that morning, and before I knew it, all the kids were filing out of chapel and on their way to the next class. I began loading up my equipment, and Robin came up and said "Here is your check for the morning, along with a second check, each is made out for $75. They said that since you did the speaking as well, you should have Jeff's check."

"No way, why don't you just give that to Jeff, it wasn't his fault he got sick." They insisted that I take the money and use it towards my music ministry. After rounds of me insisting and them insisting, I finally gave in. I did need the cash after all.

I remember driving home thinking, "WOW, I can't believe I just made $150 by doing what I totally love!" My mind began to race about how to best spend my additional check for $75. Again let me stress, this was a lot of money for a guy who had just quit his day job to pursue music as a source of livelihood.

Just then, I heard that still small voice fire off in my head, "You need to give that extra $75 to your sister."

Huh? "Uh Lord, these people wanted to bless me for the work I just did, why would we rob them of that?" Honestly people, I felt the Lord remind me, "She is letting you live with her bro, (Yes, God can say bro if He wants to) and need I remind you that she was believing in faith to raise money for her mission trip to Belize this summer. Give your sister the money."

I recall driving into the driveway of their home, and thinking,

"Wow, Terri and Dave have been so amazing to me, this is extra money that was handed to me today, and I should TOTALLY give this to Terri for her Belize trip that she is saving for. In fact Wayne, God is telling you to do it!" I was excited. With a spring in my step I walked up the drive and headed in the house, pumped to find Terri and give her this gift. I'll be honest, part of me kept screaming out to be selfish and keep the money. Isn't it funny how our own flesh likes to try and get us to do things that only serve ourselves? It was too late though, my mind was made up.

Just about that time, the mailman was walking by and handed me the mail. Terri wasn't home yet, so I dropped my bags off inside the door, and began to sort through the letters. I had changed my address, so I was getting a few bills and stuff at their house. Ah, the joys of school loans! This time however, there was only one envelope addressed to me in the stack of mail.

I opened it up, and to my surprise, there was a hand written note to me from a name that I didn't recognize. The letter said, "You don't know me, but I was at one of your concerts recently, and I was really encouraged by your songs and your message. I know this sounds a little weird, but I feel like God wanted me to send you this today. Thanks for your ministry!" I looked inside the envelope and there was a check made out to me for... you guessed it, $75.

My jaw hit the floor.

I felt God paint a very beautiful and simple illustration for me that day. "Give when I say give. You can't outgive me!" I'm thankful for that day, not only so much for the $75 gift that I was given by that precious woman, but more so for the fact that

God spoke very clearly and directly into my life. I was reminded that I wasn't in this thing alone. God really does go with us, walk with us, provide for us. God is at work all around us if we will only listen. God's plan all along was to bless me with a gift that day, but to also encourage me to a new level of obedience. He wanted to bless my sweet sis too!

Amazing I say.

The lesson from that day was burned into my heart. I don't always follow Him the way I should, I don't always act when His voice speaks. Sometimes I think I don't hear anything at all! But over and over in my life He proves Himself faithful to what He told me that day, "Give when I say give, you can't outgive me. Even if nothing is given back to you, be obedient to me."

P.S. Terri and Dave did go to Belize. They started going twice a year to serve down there. At last count, they have been down there at least 17 times.

P.S.S. I want to be a better and more cheerful giver.

# MAZES

When I was a kid, I had an entrepreneurial mind.

I have memories of being in 2nd grade and doodling during class. I had discovered mazes and how to draw them. I would make crazy mazes for my friends just for fun, usually they would be inside lettering or a drawing.

One day, a girl said, "Will you make me a maze?" I'll give you my quarter!" Ahaaa... Yes. I drew her a maze for 25¢. The next thing I knew, little Sally wanted one, then Troy, then Gabriel. I had stumbled into a little business! I did get in trouble a few times at school for drawing mazes during class. Oops.

So... I wanted to include you in the fun. Now years later, I picked up my pen and drew a few little mazes. They will appear randomly throughout this book, just to give you a break from reading. I'm sure you'll get sick of hearing my jokes in here at some point, and a break will be appreciated. So grab a pencil and turn the page.

*Also please feel free to mail 25¢ to: *Wayne Kerr Music, P.O. Box... 7432..* I'm just kidding!

# cars

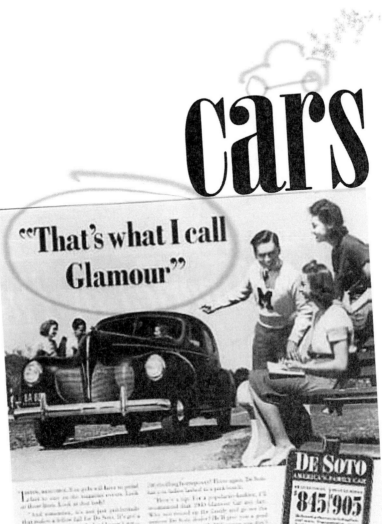

"That's what I call Glamour"

## De Soto
AMERICA'S FAMILY CAR

$845 | 905

# SOUTHLAND

I was lucky enough to receive a call to do a camp in Florida called Southland. It's a great camp run by amazing people. After the first year of doing the event, it turned into a great relationship that continued for many years doing both their Sr. High and Jr. High camps. It is held at Camp Kulaqua in central Florida. Cool name- Camp Kulaqua

The first year I was there, I did the camp solo, and the director of the camp said he would pick me up in Orlando once my plane arrived and we would go straight to the camp. It was about 2-3 hours away he said. I was pumped because it was my first opportunity with these kids and my first camp in Florida.

The night before I was to fly out, I came home and was packing up for a week of camp. My phone was blinking and there were several messages.

"Hey Wayne, I'm calling about tomorrow. It seems I have to go up early to the camp, so I'm gonna leave my car for you at the airport. It's located in the..." BEEP. End of message.

Uhhhm...

Next message: "Sorry Wayne, I got cut off... so you just go out of baggage claim and to the parking garage. In Orlando, the airport parking levels are listed by animals, so go to the BEAR level, and turn left, my car is..." BEEP. End of message.

Uhhhmm.

Next message: "Sorry bro, my car is a white beat up corolla. It's parked like 9 cars down on the first row.  If you'll look under the front bumper, you'll see I've hidden the keys there. Then as you get into the car, look in the glove compartment,  there's a map, and a bag of..."    BEEP.

Uuuuuhhhhhhmmmmmmmm...   A bag of what?

Next message: "DUDE- sorry,  a bag of quarters, cuz you'll have to go thru like 6 tollways to get to camp.  Just follow the directions and we'll see you at camp.  Oh and sorry, the AC doesn't really work."    BEEP.

# ARKANSAS STATE POLICE

In the course of this journey, I've rented vans, cars, suvs, convertibles, trucks,  and just a few months ago an infamous PT Cruiser. I'll never forget this little adventure. I was on my way to camp #9 of 11 straight weeks of camps around the country in the summer of 2009.  It was in Arkansas. I flew into Tulsa and saw my sister, Terri for a day,  then headed off to the camp. The neon blue PT Cruiser was the only thing left in my price bracket. It was a tad bright to say the least, but would work fine.

It worked fine in getting me pulled over! The officer walked up and asked me if I knew why he'd pulled me over.

"No," I said. "I was going under the speed limit I thought."

"Yes, you were," he said. "But you were swerving a little and I wanted to see if you've been drinking, or if you were over-tired."

I laughed. "I'm pretty tired alright. I've just finished 8 weeks of camps with thousands of teenagers and now I'm on my way to number 9." He didn't find me amusing.

"I need you to step out of the car Mr. Kerr. "Empty your pockets sir." "Yikes," I thought. "What the heck?" Then he asked, "Do you have any outstanding warrants?"

"No sir," I answered. I made sure that "sir" was now in every single statement I made!!!!

"Well that's funny that you say you don't, because my computer says you are wanted in the state of Michigan." At this point my heart rate was for sure up. I was trying not to freak out. "Sir, with all due respect, not only do I not have any warrants, but I've never been to Michigan in my life."

"Hmmmm, should I believe you or my computer which has never been wrong?"

I couldn't believe what he said next. "Step away from the vehicle, I need to search it. Keep your hands out of your pockets and don't think about running off, because I have a K-9 in my car, and he will run you down."

I wish I was making this story up you guys. Even now as I'm typing it I can't believe how that whole thing went down. I stood outside of my car on the side of the highway for not 20, not 30 or 45 minutes, but for an hour and a half! This officer took every single thing out of the car. Luggage, seat covers, everything. Every few minutes he would go and sit in his car, make

another call, come back, look around. It was crazy. I was thinking to myself, "If I get to make one call from jail should I call my
wife, or should I call the camp and let them know I was in
prison!?"

Finally, he said, "This will all go a lot smoother if you just tell
the truth and admit that you have a warrant out for your arrest.
I believe people can change." Wow.

"Sorry... (I had now omitted the sir. ) that's not me."

Finally, he let me go.

Be warned. If you drive thru Arkansas in a rented PT Cruiser
that's neon blue, you may have the chance like I did to be
accused of something you never did, or maybe even test your
sprint pace against a german shepherd.

# RED CONVERTIBLE

One time I flew into St. Louis, Mo. and the church hosting the
retreat said they would have someone pick me up at the airport.
I let them know that I would be flying with a guitar, keyboard in
a large flight case, pedal board, clothes bag and 2 boxes of product, just so they knew to pick me up in a van or something. "No
problem," they said.

When I arrived, a young college girl was standing there holding
a cardboard sign with my name on it in the baggage area. We
exchanged hellos, I got my gear loaded onto a cart and out we

went to her vehicle. She was driving a convertible red mustang. So we proceeded to max out that little car. We had to leave the top down with my guitar and keyboard both standing up in the back. Somehow we made it all fit, as long as I rode with my clothes bag in my lap. It didn't help that we only had about an hour and a half to drive with the top down, and it was a freezing 41 degrees outside.

# one liners you wouldn't believe

Sometimes it takes a page or 2 to tell a story. But often it's those "one liners" that stick out in my mind the best. Here is a small sampling of ones that pop into my mind over the past few years.

"You ARE having a bad hair day!" - little girl in Durango, Co.

"Hey Wayne, talk to the palm cuz you ain't the bomb." - a little girl at a camp somewhere... Ah the love.

At a camp in Florida this girl ran up to me and randomly stated, "I like pie!!!" Sweet.

After a concert in Japan, a young girl walked up and said, "I want to say in English." She said something I'll always remember, not as a thing to honor me in any way, but a testament to how powerful God is and how He inhabits praise. She said, "You sing,... heaven open,.. my heart." Wow. That was a total Holy Spirit moment that I will remember all of my days.

"Come follow me" -Jesus

"Im sorry, you don't have what it takes to be a solo artist in the Christian industry." - a manager I will leave unnamed - 1994.

"You can do anything you want to with your life." -My mom

"Get out of bed you lazy butt!" - My dad


At a camp in Nebraska, a young girl had my cd in her hand and walked up and asked if I had a sharpie. "Sure," I said with a smile on my face. "Great, cuz I want your wife Kelley to sign my CD for me."


"I'd like to introduce Wayne Kerr, one of Houston's best kept secrets." -Susan O'Donnell at a KSBJ Radio staff event


"Hey, you in the hat, get off the stage!!!" - a lighting guy screaming at me while tech people were setting up at Reliant Arena for a big New Year's Eve event I was playing.


As I said earlier, most summers for me are spent leading worship at camps, sometimes even 10 or 11 weeks in a row all around the US. Most of these camps have been Jr. high or Sr. high type events, but sometimes I get to do children's camps. These are suuuuper fun for me, kids are truly amazing. These have been the locations of some of my best~ I mean BEST one liners.


At one children's camp, they would have late night swims where literally hundreds of kids would all pile into the swimming pool. I think at camps and events like these, the worship leader and speaker have GIANT targets on their backs. After I got in the pool, I was quickly jumped by about 15-20 boys, all 3rd-4th graders. "Dunk me!" I'd dunk one. "Throw me!!" I'd toss him... "You can't flip me!" "Dunk me!!!" "My turn!!" "Dunk me!",

"Throw me!!" Then one little kid screamed, "Play me like a guitar!" What? That one I didn't know what to do with. Time to get out of the pool.

At a camp, after walking off the stage they said, "Give it up for Wayne one more time you guys!" Everyone cheered. I walked into the guy's restroom in the back of the room to wash my hands. This one little guy looked up to me and said, "Hey, you know there are alot of people way more famous than you!" "I know." I said with a smile on my face. "There sure are."

On one occasion, I had four little kids on stage to help me with a tune, and afterwards told them to take their seat. 3 of the 4 sat down, but one little boy turned and mumbled something to me. I couldn't hear him, so I said, "What was that buddy?" With a very determined look on his face he said, " I want some ice!!" I dunno.

At a youth event in Louisiana, I had kids greet each other and tell each other their first and middle names. Then I asked them, "If you could have any super hero power, what would you have?"

I asked one guy what he picked. He said, "I'd have the power to give people diarrehea!" Interesting.

One time I was playing in Japan at an Air Force Base. I was inspired by all the macho freedom fighting guys with crew cuts in the room. I looked at my wife and said, "I want to go the base and get my hair completely buzzed by one of the barbers here!"

To which she replied... "Do you really want that much of your face to show?"

"I really don't like your music too much, but if you keep paying me I guess I'll keep playing with you." - bass player who was completely honest with me. I actually appreciated it.

"How do you get your hair to be so light and fluffy?" -6th grade boy at SkyRanch.

"Wayne, listening to your music makes me want to be a better mom. Will that quote get me in your book?" - Becca

In 2001, I did a Houston area release event for my CD "Apple Core." We were fortunate to do the event at 2nd Baptist Church at their west campus. This is a great venue in the round. At that time my wife, Kelley, and I were just dating and she came into town for the CD release. It was an amazing night, there were about 1400 people there. About half way through the concert, I took a moment and wanted to introduce my family to the audience. "Right over here are my mom and dad!" Everyone cheered! "Here's my sister Terri!" Everyone cheered. Then I said, "And right there next to them, this is Kelley, my girlfriend." There was a slight hush over the crowd, and the feelings of disenfranchised pre-teenage girls became apparent. A few rows behind Kelley, she said she heard one little girl say, "I hate his girlfriend." YIKES.

Once on a mission trip to Belize, we stayed at a questionable hotel. It was intense. It was my first time to stay in a hotel where there were 8 foot walls covered with barbed wire all around them. In fact, the top of the wall had pieces of broken glass placed into the concrete. I asked, "Why are there shards of glass on the wall at the top?" "To keep people from climbing over." I was told. Gulp.

The day we were leaving we saw 3 very blonde men and women, almost Scandinavian looking. I said, "hello." I asked what they were doing down there. As they loaded several unmarked bags into a dark tinted van, one of them turned to me and answered in a thick accent almost like Arnold Schwarzenegger. "We... have a business."

I didn't want to know what kind of business he was looking so serious about, but for the rest of that trip "We have a business." was our main catch phrase.

My band and I flew to upstate New York to play at an amazing event called 4word. We flew to Newark, NJ. from Houston. Then we had to catch a smaller flight to Syracuse. The connecting plane was a smaller propeller plane, but still seated 60 people. Abe Orta Jr.(amazing drummer, keyboardist, and all around good guy) was sitting with me in the front row. We were about to take off, when the stewardess came and said the most awesome thing to me. "Sir, do you mind moving to the back row of the plane, we need to even out the weight distribution." I looked down at my belly and thought, "Have I gained that much weight?"

Before taking the stage at a Catholic youth event, a priest asked me, "Excuse me young man, but were you planning on brushing your hair before you sing?"

sound systems

We have had so many crazy experiences with sound systems over the years. The quality of the sound system has a huge impact my the level of stress and when you travel, you are left at the mercies of whoever is hosting the event. Since I am (as you know) not a big-time artist, often we get what we get. It's pretty surreal sometimes to go from one place that has amazing pro-gear and qualified people running it, to a place the next day that has the exact opposite. It's all good though. Thank goodness God is glorified either way. Honestly, He is honored when we humble ourselves for His work to be accomplished no matter if there are quality monitors on the stage or not. Still though, that being said, I've had some crazy moments that I'll never forget.

# FIRE

At camp in Mountain Home, Ga., we were in the middle of our set, bringing the rock, and we looked over and there was smoke coming over the stage. I remember thinking, "Hey I don't remember them having smoke machines for the lights!" Well sure enough, one of the sub woofers had caught on fire during the set! Some men came rushing to the stage and carried it out of the building with smoke going everywhere. Then a hush came over the audience. As they all realized we had caught the sound system on fire, one by one they began to scream like crazy. Yea we rock. I said into the mic, "It's no big deal you guys, we catch sound systems on fire all over the country."

# AWES⬤ME

A few weeks before my band was flown out to do a chapel service at University in west Texas,, I emailed them our basic sound
system needs. It listed that we fly with our instruments, but they
must provide drums, bass amp, electric guitar amp, piano, and
the appropriate mics. They said, "No problem, we will have all
that for you guys."

When we pulled up to the university, we walked into this pretty
big auditorium that seats 2000 or so. One of the reps from the
school welcomed us, and led us to the load-in area. He said,
"There were a few things on your list that we weren't able to get
for you guys."

We looked at the stage, and it looked pretty bare. He said, "We
have a great DW drum kit that's worth like $3000, but we don't
have any of that other stuff you asked for. Eeeep. It was pretty
awesome to hear my electric guitar plugged in direct, Frodo's
guitar plugged in direct, and bass direct with no pre. (That's
sound lingo for "not a good scenario.")

All you need to know is that we sounded BAD. The drums
sounded good. We did not. The ministry still went on, which is
obviously the most important thing, and I believe God was still
at work. Even though most of the students were looking at us in
disbelief. Oh yea, I sold like 1 CD.

# G⬤⬤D TIMES

One time in Missouri I showed up for a youth event in a gym.

Kids were filing in, filling up the bleachers. I looked around and saw no sound system at all. The people who booked me had insured me they had a good sound system and it would be provided. All I could see was an empty gym floor with 1 lonely mic stand standing in the middle of the court.

Someone from the facility said, "Oh yes, we have a sound system. No problem, it's up there!" As he pointed, I glanced up and saw the 2 little 1950's style horns in the ceiling. Basically, the kind used to announce basketball games. Gulp?

I just remember trying to sing and my voice sounding like muffled muffly garbeldy goop. Kids were looking at me the way my dog looks at me when he doesn't understand what the heck I'm saying. You know that look. Slight glaze of the eyes, head turned to the left ever so slightly. Yep. The night was iffy, I sold 1 CD. (I see a pattern forming here.)

As my friend Randy Guikema says, "Good times".

# REVERB

We were playing a few years ago at a cool young adult conference called Divine Rhythm. I was blessed to do several years in a row with them, and every time I was blown away by so many amazing people I met.

The last year we did the event, it was held in Gatlinburg, Tn., at a venue called "The Country Tonite Theater". If you've ever been to Gatlinburg, you probably know what the area looks like.

It's the playground of the south.Nascar, mullets and camouflage are in no short supply. Honestly, every time I have gone there it has been a blast. It's amazingly beautiful there. The venue was pretty incredible, and all through the spring and summer months it hosts it's own country show seen by thousands of people.

The venue had a lot of great gear for us and very capable sound guys. But there was one weird issue. The keyboard they had for me was nice, but it was missing the sustain pedal. It's really hard to play anything and make it sound good without a sustain pedal. (All you piano types know what's up.)

One of the sound guys said, "We'll find one and have it here by the time the event starts tonight."

"Cool." I said. "No worries."

We went through the sound check, making sure all the levels were ok. Drums, bass, acoustic, electric guitar, mics. Then we got to the piano. I went ahead and played and tried to not sound like I was in the 3rd grade. It sounded pretty choppy to say the least. The guys I play with were laughing at me. I thought, "Man, thank goodness they will have a pedal here tonight, or that would be pretty embarrassing."

We left to get settled into the hotel. We chilled from the long travel day, got changed, and came back up to the theater. People were now filing in by the hundreds, and there was a tangible excitement in the air. We were about to start, when I looked across the stage from behind the curtain, and I guess you'll imagine what I saw, or in fact didn't see. Yes, no pedal under the keyboard.

I went and asked our sound guy if they'd found a pedal. He said with his thick southern accent, "Nope, we couldn't findya one. But it sounded fine when you were sound checkin' earlier."

"We'll just throw some reverb on there, no one'll know." This became the mantra for our band for the next 2 or 3 years if anything went bad sound system wise...

"It's ok, we'll just throw some reverb on there."

# POWER OUTAGE

Once on a mission trip to Belize, we took our own sound system for multiple outdoor outreach events. One night we were to set up and play in a small town square. People began coming out of the woodwork as we set up our gear on the outdoor stage. Most people were just curious who these crazy Americans were, and wondered what we were up to.

There was noise all around, lights hung across streets and gazebos, people were everywhere. We fired up the sound system, checked it all out, and rolled into our first song. People started really gathering at this point. We were only about 30 seconds into song #2 when it happened.

The power went off.

I'm not talking about just the sound system. I'm not talking about our little light show. I'm talking the power went off in the entire town. A sonic type "boom" was heard and everything went black. "Uh oh," I thought. "Did we just blow the power in an entire city?" Yes. Yes we did.

People on our team started praying right then, that God's plan for the night would prevail, and nothing the enemy wanted to do could distract us. The power came back on.

The night was amazing. Several people accepted Christ. I'll never forget that moment when everything went black! So insane.

In a few people's lives however, the light came on that night.

# AUNT GLADYS

My sweet Aunt Gladys was being honored at her church. During a Valentines Day event she was the guest of honor. At 90 she was sweet as could be and lived an amazing life honoring the Lord. After they talked all about her inspiring life, how she rode in a biplane, moved to DC as a young adult, took cars on joy rides without the owner knowing. When they announced her as the Valentines Queen, she took the podium. Gently lifting the microphone in her hand, and placing it instead of to her mouth, straight to her ear, she sweetly said, "All I hear is crackling, I don't hear anything."

HAVE GOD AND GUITAR ...WILL TRAVEL

# BUCKLE UP

In my life God uses the in-between times, the normal day-to-day stuff to teach me great things. Just like when we are at camps and conferences, more authentic ministry often happens off the stage with kids more often than it does while we are up there leading or performing.

God calls us to lay down our lives, just as Christ laid His down for me. God really used the following story to show me just how far He has gone to serve me, and that I need to do that for others in my life.

Kelley and I moved from Houston out to Katy, a suburb about 20 miles out of town. She had been hired as the Jr. High Youth Pastor of Grace Fellowship.

I had not done a good job of getting to know our neighbors. Kelley, I will humbly admit, is WAY better at all of that. She is in fact a beautiful social butterfly.

I was pulling into our neighborhood one day, and I noticed a huge moving truck parked in front of our next door neighbor's house. As I pulled in, I got out of my truck and saw Sean out in front of his house. "What's up?" I asked him.

"I got a job back in my hometown in Michigan, and we are moving." "Wow," I said. "That's amazing bro!"

I walked in the front door of my house and very clearly I felt the Lord impressing on me a harsh truth. I had not only done a poor job of getting to know Sean and his family over the past three years, but I had missed opportunities to share about how

Christ had changed our lives. I almost audibly heard God say in my heart, "Whatever he asks of you, help him."

I figured this might be my last chance to share any moments with Sean, so I walked outside and just simply mentioned, "If there's anything I can do to help you guys with your move just let me know!"

He said, "Great, thanks!" Feeling like a good Christian guy, I walked back into my house to get back to work.

About 20 minutes later, there was a knock at the door. It was Sean. "Hey man, sorry to bug you, but you did mention if we needed anything..."

"Sure man, what's up?"

"Well, basically here's the thing. We rented this huge 25 foot moving truck, and everything we own is in it. My wife and the kids are already on their way up there to get settled. After we load this truck up, we need somewhere to store it. I will fly back to Michigan tonight, and work at my new job all this week, then on Friday, I'll fly back down here, get this truck and drive it all the way to Michigan. Would you guys mind if we left this truck in your driveway for this week?"

"Man, I'm sure that would be good, let me just check with the boss, and see what she says, but it should be totally fine!" After checking in with Mrs. Kerr (she obviously gave the green light) we let him know we were good to go. Later that afternoon he and his brother backed this huge truck into our driveway. It took up our entire driveway.

"Ok man," I said. "Just let me know if there is anything else I can do." I closed the front door and felt very grand about myself for being such a helpful person. A few minutes later there was a knock at the door. It was Sean again. "Hey Wayne, sorry to bug ya again, one quick question. I am flying into Houston Friday, and just realized that I don't have anyone to pick me up at the airport. Would you mind picking me up? Then I'll just grab the truck and be on my way."

I thought of how Bush Intercontinental Airport is about an hour from us. An hour there, an hour back. Then I was reminded of God's voice, "Whatever he asks of you, help him."

"Sure," I said. "I do have a recording session with some guys that day, but it should be no problem to make it happen. What time do you come in?"

"I'm not sure, my wife has the flight info up there, but I'll call you from there and let you know what time to pick me up, cool?"

"Sounds great." I gave him my cell phone number, and off he went. All throughout that week we parked on the street as we had this humongous moving truck in our driveway. Every day neighbors came by asking if we were moving.

Things were busy that week, and I didn't even think about the fact that it was Thursday night, and I still had not heard from Sean. I thought surely he would call at some point to let me know what time he would arrive. I had no clue how to get in touch with him. I was awakened by the sound of my cell phone by my bed at 8am or so (I know, musician hours) to the sound of Sean on the other end. Thinking he was going to tell me what time his flight was arriving, I was shocked when he said, "Hey man, I'm in baggage claim."

"What??" I said, "Dude, I'm like an hour away from you."

He said, "It's OK, I'll just meet you outside."

I scrambled to get dressed, and out the door. All the way to the airport I was thinking, "This is good of me to help." "I'm good." "I'm a servant." "I'm sure that God is proud of me for helping someone." It reminded me of a crazy Seinfeld episode.

An hour or so later I picked him up, and made small talk all the way back to Katy. I asked him about his new job, his new house, etc. Once we got home, he pulled the giant moving truck out of our driveway and back in front of their house. I shook his hand, and wiped my hands of the moving experience. "Good luck man," I said and closed the door. I now had about 2 hours to get ready for the recording session coming my way.

I have a small recording studio in my house. I've recorded my last 2 CD's from here but on that day, the City of Refuge band was coming over to track some stuff on their CD I was producing.

There was a knock at the door!!! Guess who? Sean. He said, "I'm sorry to bug you again, but I just have one more favor to ask. I have just a few things left here in the garage, and there is no room left in this moving truck. Could we use your truck to take this stuff over to a storage unit, and just unload it there? Then I can grab this stuff the next time I drive down." "It'll just take a few minutes." he added.

Now I was starting to get a little frustrated. But I wanted to help out and see this through to the end. I backed my truck up into his driveway and in front of his garage. We loaded up the back of my truck, I mean we LOADED it up. Filing cabinets, metal racks, furniture, all kinds of stuff. In fact most of it was standing up in my truck to get more things in there, which meant I would be able to drive 15 mph tops.

We were all loaded and he said, "Man could we swing by my mortgage company on the way to the storage? I just have to sign one paper and fax it off, it'll just take a few minutes." "You said you would help him," sayeth that little voice in my heart.

"Sure," I said. Now I felt like I had about given above and beyond what I was supposed to. At this point I only had an hour or so before the guys were coming to record. "Let's do this."

Off we went, at 15 mph. On a Friday, you can imagine how many people honked at me to either pull over or speed up. We'd gone about 10 minutes down the road (very slowly) when he yelled, "OH NO!!!"

"What's wrong?" I shouted!

"DUDE I left the key to the storage building back in the moving truck."

SOOOOoooooo.... We turned around, and at 15 mph made our way back to his house. I was trying my best to not be mad and trying my best not to let anything tip out of my truck!

We pulled into the neighborhood and he jumped out in front of his house. I sat in the truck with the engine running ready to go. He opened the moving truck door, looked through some bags, looked through some other bags, looked through some other bags. "This cannot be happening." I thought. Finally, he got back into my truck and said, "I have bad news and good news. The bad news is I left the storage unit key in Michigan. The good news is I have this hacksaw. We can just cut the lock."

Wow.

Off we went again, at 15 mph, pulled into his mortgage company on the way. While he was in there, I called the City of Refuge guys to cancel the recording since we were running late. When we finally arrived at the storage place my face was red, and I was tired of being helpful.

He tried for 15 minutes to cut through the lock on his own storage unit, and it wasn't even making a dent. It was unreal. Sawing, sawing, sawing, nothing. Then he finally got the owner of the storage place to cut the lockand we unloaded all his stuff into this storage unit. At this point, my recording day was shot, and I wasn't acting very Christ-like I'm afraid to say.

We drove back to my house at about 70mph at this point, and I pulled in front of his house. I shook his hand and said "Good luck man." My deed was officially done for the day!

As I walked into my house and my blood pressure began to go back down, I started thinking about the long drive that Sean would have before him. Also, I began to see how little my heart was truly wanting to be helpful and giving that day. I walked back outside and asked him how long it would take him to get over there to Michigan.

"According to Mapquest it would be about 22 hours," he said. "I'll try and make it as far as I can, maybe into Illinois, then I'll rest. I should get home the next day just in time to go to work on Monday."

"Wow man," I responded. "Will you be worried about all of your belongings sitting in a parking lot of a hotel while you are in there sleeping?"

"Actually, things are so tight money wise, I can't afford a hotel, so I'll just sleep in the bed of the truck."

I felt God say, "Pay for his hotel room."

I walked back into our house and rounded up all of the cash that we had. I walked back out and said, "Man, Kelley and I want to pay for your hotel It's super important that you rest on a crazy long drive like this. God has blessed us to be a blessing in this situation,  and HE wants you to know He is a good provider.  HE loves you man."

That day God needed to stretch me,  stretch my selfish heart. I needed to be reminded of just how many times HE has gone the extra mile for me. How in fact HE suffered the cross, just for me, to bring me into right relationship with God.  He reminded me that a woman washed His feet with her hair and He washed the feet of all of His disciples.

It was almost as if I had forgotten all the times that people have helped me. In fact, friends packed all of Kelley's things into a moving truck to get her to Houston and more friends helped us move into our first home. We had no means to make all of that happen ourselves. Oh man, how I have a heart that forgets so quickly.

Lord, please help my selfish heart. Help me to see others as You do. Help me to see others as more important than myself. God I pray today, that you will give me a chance to give. Please give me a heart like Yours. That I will give it all away.

# Weddings

i mean...

Yes. I've played at my share of weddings. And for whatever reason, I get more nervous singing or playing on someone's "special day" than performing my tunes in front of thousands of people. It's almost become comical now. The odds are very high that I'll mess up during a wedding. And when I say "mess up" I mean it happens in a way where EVERYONE notices."

# DEATH STAR

One wedding, I played from the balcony of the church. I was scheduled to play the keyboard and sing a few songs. As usual I was a nervous wreck. Again: wedding mode = stress mode. "Don't mess up," I kept telling myself. "This is their big day they will ALWAYS remember." "Don't mess up!"

The intro music went OK and I was half way home. The last song in the ceremony was one I had just learned for the wedding. Since I had not memorized the lyrics, they gave me chord charts and lyrics in a spiral binder. There was no music stand up in the balcony, so my only option was to place the binder on top of the keyboard. When I went to turn a page in the binder, it ever so gently pushed a button underneath changing the sound from 01 "Grand Piano" sound... to 00, "Death Star" sound. I wish I was sitting there with you, then I could make the sound that the "Death Star" effect emulates. Lets just say it was loud, boomy, scary, and pretty much the opposite of what a piano at a wedding should sound like.

In an instant I witnessed about 400 people turn around and look up into the balcony to see what that loud noise was. In the silence and in my humiliation, I leaned ever so gently towards the microphone, and said softly, "Sorry."

After the wedding, the bride's dad came walking quickly towards me, "Hey boy!!" I thought, "Im gonna die". He was about 6"5, cowboy, buckle, hat and all. He said, "Boy, that was one of the funniest things I've ever seen, here's an extra $20 for ya!" He patted my back really hard, and handed me twenty bucks.

# OPS

At a wedding for our friend Sharon, she asked for just a few simple tunes during the wedding. Once again, I was nervous at game time. One song at the entrance, one in the middle, and an instrumental as they exit. Should be simple right?

"Don't mess up!" I told myself again. Song #1, no problem. Song #2 went beautifulyl. The song ended, and I thought, "YES, I'm almost through this wedding, and I haven't messed up! This may be a first." The only thing remaining was the exit song, which I totally felt confident about. I did notice that the volume of the keyboard was just a little too loud, so I thought to just turn it down ever so slightly on the amp just below the keyboard. I needed to wait for a good time to make the adjustment.

The pastor began the final prayer and said, "Let us all pray as the Lord has taught us. Our Father, which art in heaven..." As the prayer began, I thought this was my chance to make the quick volume change because right after the prayer, they were to be presented as husband and wife and I would play the exit music then. "Hallowed be Thy Name..." I leaned down to adjust the amp and for no reason at all, my left hand just slammed onto the keys of the piano. "Thy will be done on earth as it is in... BLLLAALAAAAAANNNNNNG!

Everyone jumped. The pastor. The bride. The groom. The bridesmaids. The little children. Grama and Grampa. Everyone. They all looked at me with the expression you might imagine. I thought, "You've got to be kidding me."

Need I continue?

No, I didn't sing at my own wedding! Weddings and Wayne go together with fear and trembling.

# OOPS AGAIN

A few years later, I got another chance to redeem myself. A young lady called who had heard my music growing up in youth group. She asked me to sing for her on her special day. With a slight gulp in my throat, I accepted. "Just don't mess up bro!" I told myself.

This wedding was held in Houston. It was at a beautiful place. The room where the wedding was to happen was really small, maybe seating 80 people at the most. Since it was so small, really no sound system was needed. (Good for me!) There was a piano in the room I could use. The bride's mother had let me know of the songs selected. The bride wanted me to do Canon in D. She like the arrangement I did for my Christmas CD that had come out a few years before. She said, "My daughter is just dying to hear Canon in D as she walks down the aisle."

People started arriving, and were all seated. I was playing instrumental music. Then came time for the entrance of the wedding party. I began to focus all my energies on playing the best Canon in D that I had ever played. If this young lady wanted to hear my version of it, I needed to bring the very best... beyond 100%. As I was playing, I noticed the bride's mother on the front row whispering something my direction. "What?" I gently mouthed back. She replied again while shaking her head back and forth in the international symbol for "NO."

"What are you saying?" I mouthed back.

She shouted "NOT THAT SONG YET!!!" Everyone jumped.

Oops. As it appeared, I was playing the Canon in D while the bridesmaids were to be walking in. I quickly changed to some instrumental music while they finished walking in. Yikes. When I saw the bride, I started the Canon over again.

Just a fair warning to you if you are a teenage girl dreaming of having me play at your wedding someday. Weigh out the consequences carefully my friend, you may get more than you bargained for.

PS- Recently Tommy and Betty, long-time friends of mine wanted me to sing at their daughter's wedding. Jeni was like 10 years old when I started doing music ministry and now in her 20's she was getting married. Good news! I made it through with no mistakes! In all honesty, it was such an honor and a true blessing to be a part of this special day.

One of the joys of ministry is to watch over a period of time how the Gospel of Christ truly impacts a life. What was even more amazing, the ceremony was conducted by Ben Trammell. He was also a youth that I knew back in the day, and is now a Pastor at Lakewood UMC in Houston. Amazing.

MUSIC MINISTRY STORIES PART 2

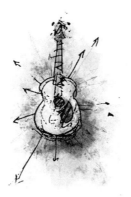

# YAHIRA

This is her name. We met when I was on a mission trip to Costa Rica several years ago. I went with a church from Carrollton, Tx. who did ministry down there every year. We were on a mission to build a church building from scratch, right after we cleared a thorny field.

She was a sweet little girl, maybe 10 years old or so, and we sure hit it off that week. Every day 80-90 kids would come around and play games. Every day that number would grow it seemed. Yahira hung around me whether I was playing with kids, or working on the septic tank. Yes, I was over the septic tank digging team... why they picked me for that I'm not sure.

Little boys would be playing soccer in this overgrown nasty field. One time I remember one little boy just stopped in mid-game and started to pee out in the field. WHOA I thought, "Things are mucho different down here!"

A night that sticks out in my mind was when the church building was actually taking shape with simple walls. That night we had the very first worship service to ever be held in the small building. There were no windows and no roof, and it was awesome. Hundreds came and crammed in there, some stood outside looking through the open squares that might one day have window panes in them. They ran extension chords and hung 2 light bulbs up in the middle of the room. As you might imagine: Costa Rica + nightime + jungle + lightbulb =  mosquitos and bugs like crazy!

As we sang worship songs together I remember thinking, "If you tried to have a church service in the US in these conditions, people would be complaining about the heat, the bugs, the lighting, and would most likely leave." I remember the faces of these precious people singing their hearts out! They FINALLY had a church of their own! It was beautiful.

The day we were leaving, I saw Yahira. She was crying. Since my spanish was pretty rough, I spoke to her through a translator. "Don't be sad! God loves you so much and we will come back, I promise!" I asked the translator for her address and maybe we could stay in touch. She cried more and said something to the worker, which was translated, "You cannot write to her. The streets have no names, and the houses don't even have numbers. There's no mail service like that here." Wow. Before I left I said, "I want you to have this!" I gave her my guitar pick. (It was all I could find as a small gift.) She smiled and we hugged.

One year later, I returned with the same team. I remember so vividly as our bus pulled into the town hundreds of kids came running and screaming all around. It was like the Jonas Brothers had arrived to an Orlando mall or something. I walked off the bus and was giving hi-fives and hugs. Next thing you know I saw Yahira, another year older, now 11. The smile on her face was about a mile wide. We hugged each other, and she said "¡Espéreme por favor!" (Please wait). She pulled out her little bag and was looking through it, giggling. Then she pulled out the guitar pick I had given her over a year ago. She just wanted me to know she still had it.

That moment will stick with me always. The smallest gift from the heart means so much. We had not only taken supplies, construction, fun games, and septic tank digging tools to Costa Rica. We had taken the very heart of Jesus Christ to those people. I pray for Yahira today that she is still walking with Him.

Another strong memory from that trip was a really hot day, well over 100 degrees. We were all outside working. Kids were playing and having fun. Every couple hours or so we would all take a water break. Our teams would all grab bottled water, because we could not drink the water there.

The kids would all get in line for the water hose. There were tons of kids everywhere. I was sitting to the side, and I saw a little bitty girl, maybe 4 years old, trying to get to the hose through many kids. She kept getting bounced back in line or pushed aside by bigger children. The moment when I was about to get up and go take her some water, I saw something. Her older sister sat her down over in the shade. The older girl went over to the line, stood in line in the heat, and when she got to the hose, cupped her hands together and filled them full of water. She walked directly to her little sister, and I watched the little girl drink from her sister's hands. I couldn't believe what I was seeing. Again she returned to stand in line in the heat, waiting. Cupping her once more, she brought water to her sister.

We as believers know the source of liver water. We have tasted and seen that the Lord is good! Psalm 34:8. We have tased forgiveness, refreshment, new life. Why in the world would we not cup our hands together, and take it to someone who needs it?

# THE U. N.

I caused a big argument on the floor of the General Assembly at the United Nations.

During my senior year of college, my Art professor, John Nellermoe (amazing guy by the way) suggested I enter some of my art pieces into a few national competitions. I agreed to check it out. He was always passing cool things along to me, magazines of art galleries and information on upcoming competitions. I was trying to keep a pulse on the art world and what work people were up to out there.

One of the competitions that struck a chord with me was through the Albert Schweitzer Foundation. For those of you who just said, "Albert who?" Do yourself a favor and hit him up on Wikipedia or Google. He was a German theologian, musician and author who in the 1920's and 30's came to a crisis of belief in his faith. He struggled deeply with his faith, and how to put his faith to any action. God had led him to Africa to help the needy and literally start a hospital. What's funny is, he wasn't a doctor. He was so compelled it was of the Lord (and his conscience many say) that he went to medical school. He went on to travel to Africa, and over the course of his life, launched several hospitals, treating over 500,000 people in his lifetime. He was given the Nobel Peace Prize. The main hospital continues to serve and treat people today.

I decided to do an illustration for this Schweitzer competition. One winner from each state would be chosen. I did a large illustration in charcoal, black and white. It was a collage of images. Schweitzer's face, the continent of Africa, a black hand and white hand embracing. I thought it was pretty cool.

We took photos of the piece and sent it in. I didn't think much about it as the year got moving along. Three months later, Mr. Nellermoe called me into his office and said I had a piece of mail. When I opened it I was shocked to read that I had won the

Texas position in the contest. Not only that, I would be flown to New York in the spring for an event called the Albert Schweitzer Colloquium. Students from all over America and the world would be there for the event. I was floored. My professor was pumped. My parents were amazed.

Off I went to New York! I had never been there before. I thought, "Hey I'm from Houston, it's pretty big, how different could New York be?" Yikes. I was way off.

I remember on the plane ride there, I sat next to a really awesome Jamaican lady who lived in New York. In the early 90's crime was still pretty high in NY. She was hilarious, giving me all these safety tips.

"Don't look up in de air child... if'n you do it, they'll be like - Oh he's from outa town!!"

"Keeps your wallet der in ya front pocket child... dat way if'n you have a pickpocket, they won't get every-ting."

By the time we arrived, I don't know if I was comforted or freaked out. On the shuttle ride through New York, I remember thinking, "This guy is driving crazy!" All around me cars were honking. Everyone seemed to be honking at each other all the time.

As we were swerving in and out of traffic, the driver simply forced his way into another lane, cutting off this taxi cab. They nearly wrecked. I looked around the shuttle and people were all reading the paper, reading books, or looking out the window showing no emotion. Next thing I knew, we came to a stop light, and the taxi driver pulled up next to the shuttle and got out of his taxi. He was outside the shuttle cussing up a storm at the driver. Before I knew it, the shuttle driver opened up the door, and bounced out to have it out with this taxi driver!!!

These guys literally got into an altercation out on the street! They were cussing each other out, pushing each other, and one guy took a few swings. Honestly, and I'm not making this up, no one on this shuttle even reacted. More like, "Oh this kinda thing happens every day." EEEP.

The guy got back on the bus, closed the door and we were on our way again. My face must have shown the international sign for "I'm from outa town." I was shocked. With wide eyes and a dropped jaw I looked around for any other human on that shuttle to be reacting the same way. I was pretty much alone. "Wow", I thought, "I don't think we are in Texas any more Toto."

The event started and we were lucky enough as college students to be given seats in the main hall of the United Nations. It was crazy. Every single chair has a small device to the lower right that has several knobs on it. You place an earpeice in your ear, and you can hear a translator. It's pretty incredible to turn the knob and go from language to language. Korean to Russian, Arabic to Spanish. I was overwhelmed with the bigness of the world we live in.

As the conference went on, I started noticing how there was a lot talk about secular subjects. Medicine, cruelty to animals, the Dr.'s work in hospitals. It was clear they were staying away from Albert Schweitzer's spiritual beliefs. One of the days there was a husband and wife who spoke, and honestly three days into this event, they were the first to ever mention that he was a Christian man. They mentioned his beliefs in Christ, and his deep desire to know Him more. They mentioned his deep questions and doubts of God. The session we were in was titled "World Peace".

They had a question and answer time where anyone could walk up to the general assembly microphone and ask questions or make a statement. For whatever reason my young heart was so stirred and inspired by this couple, I went to the mic. After a few before me, I stepped to the microphone and said, "I want to thank this nice couple for coming and sharing today and mentioning the name of Jesus. I think in a discussion about world peace, it is impossible to have that discussion without mentioning Jesus Christ."

Little did I know what was coming. Quickly a man shouted from across the room in another language, "Just because I am not Christian DOES NOT MEAN I DO NOT WANT WORLD PEACE!" Another man shouted, "What he meant was..." Another lady screamed over him, "This is the kind of attitude that..." Then all the shouting came together to where I could not clearly understand anyone.
I slowly walked back to my seat as the arguing continued. Many of the college students I was with that week all smirked and looked away, even changed seats as to not be near me.

At the time I had no idea what was even going on. Now as I look back at it, I fully recognize, there is a big world out there, and many of them do not believe the way I believe. Many of them shun Christ, many think He was just a nice guy, many think of Him as a made up fable. The reality is, here is what Jesus Himself said about the topic:

Jesus was the ultimate sacrifice for us, and still today mentioning His name can cause arguments. Even to the point of separating family members. Jesus said this 2000 years ago, and it's still true today. Who do you say He is?

Matthew 20:28 "...just as the Son of Man did not come to be served, but to serve, and to give his life as a ransom for many."

# GOD CORRECTS ME IN KANSAS CITY

Several years ago there was a national Catholic youth event to be held in Kansas City, Mo. Somehow I ended up on a list of many artists invited to play. I'm not sure how they had heard of me, not being Catholic and all. Initial estimates said that there would be approximately 10,000 kids at this weekend conference. I was so pumped to be asked to play there. My mind began to race at not only the spiritual opportunity to encourage so many students in Christ, but how it might open doors in my career. Since I had not done much in the Catholic world, I was excited to play for them, and share what Jesus has done in my life and encourage relationship with Him.

I will admit to you that as the event drew closer, my mind was less on the things of God and what He may have in store for those kids. I began to focus on how to get enough product there for that many students, just in case it went really well. I began to think of my image, I started thinking of all the gigs around the country I might get after performing there, I began to think about promoting me. It's a slippery slope in this Christian music world I have found, how to properly juggle and balance the ministry without getting wrapped up in the self-promotion. God used this event big-time to bring some correction in my life.

The closer I got to the date of the event, I was informed that I would not be singing in the main auditorium in front of 10,000 kids, but would be actually singing one of the later night options. These rooms packed 1000 kids in each. I thought, "Well that's a bummer, but 1000 kids is a lot!"

I arrived in KC, and was in the midst of a solo tour through the midwest. I loaded in all my gear during the day, and set up my product booth in the EXPO room. I had intentionally purchased additional CD's just to bring to the conference.

The night of my performance arrived. They had randomly drawn the names of the artists, I was picked to play 8th out of 10. I thought no prob! The room began to fill, the energy was amazing. Kids were hyped and going crazy. There were exactly 1000 kids in the room. Because of fire code, they would let no more in. If 5 kids walked out they would let 5 new ones enter, and there was a line outside to get in. I kept thinking, "This is gonna be amazing." I was feeling kinda full of myself as I thought I'd be the best artist they saw that night.

As time was ticking on the 6th artist was done, and the 7th taking the stage. I was up next. Just at that moment, I saw a few of the groups starting to leave. Then other groups started filing out, then in droves they were exiting the room. I asked someone what was going on. Come to find out, all the students were being bussed back to the hotels where they were staying, and those busses were leaving at 11pm. It was now 10:45.

By the time I walked onto the stage, the room that held 1000 people was down to 30, and they were turning the house lights on. I remember the sinking feeling so well. A feeling of disbelief, and a feeling of self-righteous anger flaring up in me. "Why did they even ask me to come to this?" "10,000 to 1,000, and now there's no one even in here!" I was missing the boat in so many ways it was ridiculous.

All the lights were now on, and after only 2 songs I walked off the stage. By the time my second song was over, literally the only people in the room were sound and light people, who were starting to tear down their equipment. I broke down my product table and put everything back in the boxes. All the cds, shirts, hats, and brochures promoting ME.

I had not sold a SINGLE thing. I remember with such clarity what came next. As I was rolling my cart down a back service hallway of this convention center my cart hit a small crack in the concrete, and the top heavy boxes slowly leaned forward. Today I remember it as if it were in slow motion. The front 4 cardboard boxes all tipped forward and fell. With an erie uniformity, about 800 CDs fanned out in all directions across this slippery dark grey concrete floor.

Standing there in disbelief of how the night could get any worse, I knelt down and began to pick them up one at a time. Just then I felt the HOLY conviction of our Lord. It was like my eyes were opened to see my selfishness, and I saw clearly how badly I'd been behaving, how self-centered.

Tears began to roll down my face, as I felt the regret of my motives. A few service people walked by looking at me like I was crazy, none of them stopped. This was clearly my mess to deal with. With each and every CD I picked up and put into a box, I began to hear the Holy Spirit.

"So, tonight was all about you?"

"So, I called you to this ministry to sell CDs?"

"Don't you think I might have wanted to use you to GLORIFY ME in full view of the lives of these kids that I love so dearly?"

"Have I ever let you go without, and haven't I been a good provider?"

In the same instant that I began to feel the convicting heart of GOD in that hallway, I also heard His heart of forgiveness!

"I am so proud of you, and I am for you, Wayne."

"I am the vine, you are the branch, abide in me and you will bear fruit, if you don't you won't."
"I love you."

"Come follow me."

My tears continued, but began to come from a different place. Not from a place of anger or frustration, nor from a place of guilt or regret, but now I cried from feeling so overwhelmed with HIS love for even me. With every item I picked up and but back into a box, I thought of all the many times Christ has forgiven me, picked me back up, and re-instated me for His service.

I remember the feeling deep in my heart as I was driving home from Kansas. A huge lesson that needed to be taught, a divine course in reformatting my priorities. Believe it or not, I felt SO BLESSED for the opportunity to have heard so clearly from God, even if it was a heart correction. I was reminded that HE is in fact with me, and HE is in fact for me.

Unfortunately, this is an area God has had to teach me several times. As long as there is breath in our lungs, things will be competing with the Lordship of Christ in our lives.

For you today it might be sports, feeling that if you could just be the best athlete, then you'll get all the friends, all the applause, the right scholarship. Maybe you think if you are the loudest, the funniest, the skinniest, the prettiest, the richest... on and on it goes. Ever since Adam and Eve blew it, we have all been carrying the same sin DNA. That thing that slowly creeps up and tries to convince us that we can be gods ourselves.

I pray that today you and I will both take a moment to stop. Take a moment to pray and ask the Creator of the universe, the Father, Son and Holy Spirit to reign in our hearts. Let's pray that our joy is not found in what others see in us or say about us, but rather in what HE says about us. Here are some amazing things He has to say about us.

"You are a masterpiece, created new in Jesus Christ to do great things that I have planned long ago." Eph 2:10

"Anyone who belongs to Christ has become a new person. The old life is gone; a new life has begun." 2 Corinthians 5:17

"While we were yet sinners, Christ died for us." Rom 5:8

"Do not think of yourself more highly than you ought, but rather think of yourself with sober judgment, in accordance with the measure of faith God has given you." Romans 12:3 Pride. Die in me. in Jesus' name.

# HEY THAT SHIRT LOOKS FAMILIAR

Have you ever felt wronged in some way? It can be a major league thing like a friend stabbing you in the back or a betrayal of trust. It might be someone cutting you off on the highway or a person stepping in front of you at a checkout line. Either way, you probably know the feeling.

Here is an example of something that happened to me a few months ago. A speaker friend of mine asked me to be involved with a CD compilation he was doing to raise money for orphans in Africa. Artists were donating one song each to a CD to raise funds. "Sounds great" I said. So we sent him a tune.

A few months later, I went to his website to grab a pic of the CD cover to help promote it. While I was on his site I thought I'd look around at his schedule, pics and products etc. When I went to his product page, I saw this shirt- I've blurred the name, cuz that's not important.

Here is a pic of one of my tour shirts that I have been selling for many years when I'm out on the road. Anything look similar? Yikes.

I remember the old familiar prideful feeling rise up in me, that feeling that has been around as long as humans have been on the planet. That feeling was, "Hey I've been wronged! And I am mad about it!!"

"I can't believe after that camp we did together that he would steal my t-shirt design!" My selfish mind was racing.

The Spirit of God arrived on the scene in my room. I felt Him remind me so clearly of all the MANY times He has had to forgive me and He asks me to love and forgive others in the same way! I was reminded of what Jesus had to say about the subject. Frankly, He says to forgive, and move on. That's it. Not 7 times, but 70 times 7 is what Jesus Christ said. Matt 18:21-22

That speaker and I still joke about it today. The enemy would love nothing more than for us to break relationships, to not forgive, to hold a grudge. How has Christ forgiven you, given you new life where there was none? Who can you forgive today? Pick up the phone,  send an email, walk into the next room, go hug your mom.

Forgive as Christ forgave you.

You will feel the burden lift.

You might even laugh about it later.

# JOSH AND THE FISH HOOK

One of my best friends is Josh Anderson.  Amazing guy. He's married to an amazing girl, Lori.  They have both played a major role in my ministry, especially in the early years. There were many weekends that I was out on the road going to some retreat and often Josh would come along. We would load heavy speakers and ancient gear making due the best we could.

At the end of one retreat we loaded up and got into my truck. They had done a lesson with the kids that weekend and used fish hooks as some symbolism. Josh gave me a fish hook and said, "Here man, keep this. It will remind you that you are a fisher of men."

As of today, nearly 10 years later, and several vehicles later, I still have that fish hook dug into the carpet of my truck in the center console. It serves as a constant reminder of the calling. Jesus said, "Hey you guys, come follow me, I'll make you fishers of men." Thank you, Josh.

# NEBRASKA

One of the coolest churches I've been blessed to be involved with is Westside Baptist in Omaha, Ne. I will say it's much easier to get around up there in the summer months. I flew in one time in the winter, and it must have been pretty obvious from the expression on my face that I was from the south. Ice and snow were covering the pavement just outside the door of baggage claim. In fact, the snow was blowing completely sideways. I was freaking out big time.

One time when I was booked there, I got to share a song in the main sanctuary during the service, then walk over to the children's ministry to share a message along with some tunes. My friend Charlie McAllister was the children's pastor there, amazing and crazy guy!

I was sharing the story from Mark 4:35-40 where Jesus is in the boat with his homies. They had finished a long day of ministry, you know, watching Jesus do His thing... healing people, making a guy who was blind able to see, raising the dead, a typical Jesus day. They headed out in a boat to cross the lake. Jesus went to rest, so He laid down in the boat, chillin for a nap. The weather began to get rough. Wind, rain, waves. The slightly "iffy" weather conditions soon turned into a hazardous situation.

If I had a few million dollars, I'd LOVE to make a movie or two. I can just imagine this scene on the big screen. Can you see it? The rain pounding the boat as it is tossed up and down, across and over. The ear piercing wind and howling, the fear in the eyes of the men holding on for their lives, the Savior of the world who is sleeping soundly with a slight grin on His face.

I can see the disciples telling each other one by one, "You wake Him up," "No you wake Him up, I'm not waking Him up, did you see what He did to that guy who was possessed by a demon? What if He's cranky when He wakes up?!"

Finally one of them must have lost at drawing straws or something, and was forced to wake up Jesus. "Wake up Lord, save us, we are perishing!!" Immediately Jesus rebuked the wind, almost in the same way a child is told to calm down by a loving parent who sees the kid is out of control. "Peace, be still!!" He said to His creation. The bible says at that moment the rain stopped, the wind ceased, and the waves began to mellow down until the lake itself was calm.

Again, if I were directing this movie, the camera would pan over to see 12 grown men with all of their eyes wide and jaws dropped, mouths open in awe.

Calmly, Jesus responds in that way that He often talks to me. Reassuring, yet making the moment a teachable one. "You of little faith, why is it that you were afraid?"

As I was telling this story to a room of about 400 1st-4th graders, you could see them hanging on every word of the story. I was doing my best to recreate the scene in their minds. It was pretty amazing how you could hear a pin drop in that room it was so quiet! Then I continued with building anticipation. "The disciples said, "Who is this man that even the wind and the waves obey him?"

At that very moment, in the quiet of the room, this little boy from way in the back screamed, "HE'S THE WEATHER MAN!!"

The room burst out in laughter. I was laughing too. I said, "Yep, that's pretty accurate. He's THE weather man."

Jesus can speak peace into any situation. What I can learn from this story is that He is ultimately in control and that I don't have to fear the storms in my life. Maybe today you are walking thru a stormy situation. Call on Him. Don't be afraid.

Maybe you have never asked Jesus into your boat. If you haven't, you should. Trust Him with your life. The storms of life will come, and I'd sure hate to not have Him in my boat. Maybe you are already a believer, but you need to say "JESUS, wake up in me again."

*"Tiny little hands, that will calm the sea, even the ones inside of me. Tiny little hands, will know the hammer, will know the nail too well, too well."* - lyrics from "The Carpenter" on Wayne's "Waiting for Christmas" CD

# SO GOOD

In 2005, I wrote a worship song called "So Good." It's a pretty simple song musically, but really expresses a desire to simply tell God how good, faithful and amazing He is.

*"These words are not enough, these songs are not enough, to tell You just how truly good You are."* Written from the place of saying, "You know what, just going through the motions of church on a weekly basis is not enough. Clocking in mentally for an hour, and singing a few songs isn't enough." God desires a real

relationship with me that is 24 hrs a day, 7 days per week, 365 days per year, every year of our lives! He deserves so much in response to all He has given. The chorus says: *So good, so good I just want to tell You how, so good You are.* God desires a THANKFUL heart.

I had a powerful experience with this song a few summers ago. We were leading worship at an amazing Jr. High camp down in Padre Island, Tx. There were nearly 1000 kids at the camp that week. To say there was a lot of energy in the room would be a massive understatement! Kids were hyyyypped up. It was so incredible to be with these students for 2 sessions a day.

One night as we drew near the end of our worship set, the staff informed me that the pastor was ready to go after the next song. The young lady who was overseeing the production end of the event asked me to instruct the kids to all be seated for the last song to begin in order to set the stage for the message. After all the kids were seated, we began to launch into "So good." I had just written the tune a few months before, and this was one of my first attempts at doing it live.

God inhabits the praises of His people. It's just that simple. When people, young or old, take their eyes off of themselves and direct their attention, praise and worth to God, He responds. He receives it. He enjoys it. I'm not sure how to describe it, but somehow in the process, the people are then blessed too. It's what we were created for after all.

One by one, kids started standing all over the auditorium, till once we had reached the last chorus of the song, the entire room was standing and singing. I remember as the song ended, we were just repeating the chorus only, with no instruments, just their voices. It was amazing on so many levels. Not only was it so humbling to hear all those kids singing the song that was just coming from my heart, but it was inspiring to see that even if you tell tons of kids to be seated and God is at work in them, they will still stand in His presence.

I remember it was one of the most tangible times in my ministry where the presence of God was felt so near. The band and I walked off the stage and none of us said a word to each other. I remember that I was overwhelmed, and just tried to hold off the tears... Randy Harvey went straight to his bible... Raymond Turner went straight to his journal... it was awe inspiring.
He is good. He does inhabit the praise of His people. Psalm 22:3 He wants to live there.

The song "So Good" came from an honest outpouring from me to God. It's been unreal to hear students and churches out there singing it. It is so sweet to hear others connect to God through singing a simple song God had given me.

I'd only written the chord progression on piano, and had no words or melody. For whatever reason it just felt worshipful, and I almost couldn't play it without crying every time. I recorded just the piano part, and bounced it down to a CD to take with me on an out of town trip with my wife. We flew to New Mexico to see her family, got a rental car, and began our two hour drive.

An hour or so into the drive, she fell asleep in the passenger seat, and I put the disc in just to listen to some of the music ideas. I just began to worship and thank God for His faithfulness. Even as I looked over at my wife asleep, I became overwhelmed, and the tears started flowing down. Hey guys, don't laugh. I grabbed a napkin, and wrote out the lyrics while the music played in the cd player.

*lyrics:*

These words are not enough
These songs are not enough
to tell You just how truly good You are

A song is just a song
These words are empty if
My heart is hardened to who You are

So Good,  So Good
So Good I just want to tell You how
So Good, So Good You are

Brighter than the morning star
Faithful thru the ages
Father to all generations
Listen to the song we sing
You are everlasting, Holy, Indescribable

So Good, So Good,
So Good I just want to tell You how
So Good, So Good You are.

# TWELVE THOUSAND

That's the number in attendance of the largest event that I've
played at. It was Youth '03, in Knoxville, Tn. I was lucky enough

to be playing at a few smaller side events during the event, and I was also asked to open for Kirk Franklin on the main stage. I pretty much knew that whatever I did on stage was about to be blown away by Kirk and his killer band. Not only was his band amazing, but he had like 15 vocalists who were all over the top!

Opening for Kirk Franklin was pretty fun to say the least. It was surreal to be looking out at a basketball arena full of students. Right after my set, I walked off stage and sat just to the side of the stage at about 20 rows up to watch Kirk. I remember watching an amazing and anointed entertainer and minister do his thing.

I also remember thinking, "That was really amazing that I just got to do that... perform in front of so many kids. If you would have asked me a few years ago about it, this moment should be the highlight of my career!

I remember sitting there, reflecting on those 15 minutes. I realized that I am truly just as happy and satisfied when I am sitting in my house on my couch with my amazing wife & best friend ,Kelley, and our dog."

It was a comforting moment in my heart, when I realized that my joy was not found in success or failure in the music world, or based on what any person thinks or doesn't think of me. My joy comes from HIM, and my family is a gift from the Father.

# ROOM FOR FOUR

I was booked to play in Sarasota, Florida by a great friend of mine, Mike Tisdal. This guy really loves the Lord and has been so great to bring me in to different churches over the years. From Tampa I was to connect to Sarasota on a smaller plane. I walked through the terminal in Tampa looking at my boarding card trying to find my connection. Some airline folks directed me down some stairs, along a hall, and into another waiting area.

Outside the windows I could see some reeeealllyyy little planes parked outside. I thought, "Whew... I'm glad Im not flying on one of THOSE today." You can guess what's coming next. Yep. I knew that the little plane I was looking at was about to be my ride when I saw a guy trying to fit my guitar into a little compartment on the wing of the plane just behind the propeller. Yikes.

The attendant told me to step up to a scale. Since there are only 4 seats on the plane, yes four, they said they needed to balance the passengers out according to weight. Huh?

Onto the scale I went. "That thing is off a little bit" I joked. She didn't laugh. As my sweet wife, Kelley, often has to say to me, "Not everything has to be funny, Wayne."

They even weighed my backpack. Yikes. Outside we went, onto the tarmac. We climbed into the little plane, and the pilot said, "Uhm you sit here, and I guess... you sit here."

Gulp.

After a few nervous moments, the pilot fired up the engine. It was pretty funny because NO ONE was talking on this little plane. I think all (four) of us just wanted to live to see Sarasota.

Let me say, when I'm flying I prefer to NOT see all the controls of the aircraft. I prefer to NOT hear the pilot asking for clearance and wind speeds. I'd rather sit in my comfy metal tube, turn a movie on and pretend we aren't going 575 miles an hour at 30,000 feet in the air. This trip was the exact opposite of that.

We were gently rolling down the runway to get in line to take off, when the pilot took off his headset and said to us, "It's pretty warm in here, let me turn on some air conditioning for you folks." At which point he literally opened the side window as he busted out laughing. Ok, I'm thinking, less comedy routine bro, more flying. Maybe Kelley is right. Not everything has to be funny.

Since the pilot was in his mid-70's, long straggly moustache and super thick glasses, I thought, "I'd better look over his shoulders and see what the controls are just in case this guy has a mid air heart condition." (That's horrible I know.) Altimeter... check. Fuel gage... check. Spinning dial thing... check. Other cool emergency lever dealy... check. I was all set in case I needed to take over.

Up we went. If you've ever flown in one of these little Cessna planes, you know how loud it actually is in there. You also know how much the plane seems to move around, drifting left, right, down, up, down and left again..

Eeeeesh.

This flight was to only be about 25 minutes or so, and I thought,

"I can totally do this." We were only up about 3000 feet, and it actually was a great view of the Tampa Bay area. Beautiful. About half way through the trip, you could already begin to see the runway appearing ahead. It was at this point that the nerves began again. "Left, no more left, straighten it out, not too much" was all going thru my head. It appeared this guy had never landed before in his life! Closer and closer we edged, until finally we heard and felt the sound of our landing gear touching down on the landing strip.

At that very moment we could see emergency vehicles scrambling on the runway, lights flashing, sirens blaring. I didn't know what was going on! "Is our plane on fire?" I wondered. As we all looked out of the plane to our left, we saw that another Cessna plane, same size as ours, had just made an emergency landing. It's nose was in the ground and tail in the air. None of us were saying anything at this point!

As we slowly rolled to a stop, they lowered the ladder for us to de-plane. Several attendants from the airline were there to greet us and welcome us to Sarasota, almost as if they didn't see the smoke rising 300 feet away. I got off the plane and literally kissed the ground. Once again, the stewardess wasn't laughing at all, she looked at me like I was an idiot.

After I got my luggage, I immediately called and cancelled my next "Cessna" connecting flight back to Tampa, and I walked straight to the car rental desk.

# FIRST CLASS

I've only flown 1st class one time, and it was because I got bumped. Yep, I'm not sure how that happened actually. It was another small blessing from a time of going to serve others. I was on my way to Costa Rica on a mission trip, and when I got to the airport, they told me the flight was over sold. Hmmmm... I still don't understand how airlines do that. Don't you have a certain number of seats?

The attendant behind the counter said, "This is your lucky day. Coach is over booked, but it looks like we have one open seat, and it's in first class."

"If I have to, I have to." I said.
As we loaded onto the plane, I saw pretty quickly the draw of first class. Huge seats, nice leather, pillows, tv screen, hot hand towels. Ahhhhhh. Even the peanuts arrived in high class. Not in a little wrapper, but a fancy little jar.

The man sitting next to me seemed like a high roller. I asked him what he did, and he said he was the regional director for Coca-Cola for all of Mexico, Central and South America. Cool. The attendant came by and offered us a Pepsi, he declined.

# INDONESIAN AIRPLANES

A few years ago, Kelley and I were lucky enough to go to Indonesia and minister there with a small team. It's so amazing when you fly internationally, because even when you go into the international terminal in Houston, you begin to see all the cultures change. You hear the different languages in the air, and you start to see that everyone around the world doesn't dress at all the same. I live a pretty sheltered life sometimes here in the US, I'll admit.

Our first flight was from Houston to LA. The attendant made all the announcements on the plane in english. Our next flight was LA to Tokyo. They made half the announcements in english, and half in Japanese. Our next flight was from Japan to Indonesia. The messages were Japanese, then Indonesian, then something else that I had no clue as to what it was. There was no announcement in English. It's a strange feeling when you hear an aggressive sounding announcement over the speaker in the plane, and you have no clue if he said, "Prepare for an emergency landing" or "We are about to begin our beverage service."

Coming into Indonesia, it was rough weather, actually some of the bumpiest I'd ever been through. Lighting, rain, wind, it was crazy. I was doing a lot of praying as I recall.

We landed safely, though not smoothly. As we exited the plane, it was late at night in Indonesia, and rain was coming down in buckets. I could see giant palm trees swaying in the storm. I also saw armed guards with machine guns all around the small airport. We walked into the terminal and there was only one baggage claim carousel. Written above it in english and in HUGE block lettering, "**NO DRUGS ALLOWED, PUNISHABLE BY DEATH.**"

On our last leg of the trip, we were going on an Indonesian airline from one city to a smaller one to reach our final destination.

As we were in the terminal to board the next plane, it seemed that everyone was really antsy to get on board. People were almost jockeying for position to be the first on the plane. We were trying to figure out what was up, when our friend Danny said, "Many Indonesians have never flown before. For most of these folks, they have spent much of their lives traveling by boat or rickshaw. People line up far in advance, and try to be the first ones on the boat just to make sure they have a place. They don't really understand that with the ticket they have, they are already guaranteed a seat on the plane."

So as the doors opened for us to walk out on the tarmac, sure enough, many people started running to the plane, feeling the need to push each other out of the way, it was wild. Then we boarded the plane by climbing up a small skinny ladder that came down out of the rear of the aircraft.

Yikes.

A different travel culture for sure. A beautiful people too.

RANDOM CONCERT HAPPENINGS

# TELL THEM WHAT?

One of the things I love about performing live is that you NEVER know what might happen. Sometimes things go just according to plan. Sometimes the exact opposite happens.

A few years ago I was playing an outdoor community-wide event. It was being held in a town square. There were local bands, singers, some secular, some from churches, etc. After singing a few of my tunes, I shared how amazing God is and how I hoped that if anyone was in reach of hearing my voice, they would consider giving their hearts to Him today. Just then, a tug at my feet from the bottom of the stage, revealed an elderly man who was involved with the event. Cowboy hat, wrinkled skin, total country guy.

He interrupted my invitation to know the love of Christ and asked me to make an announcement over the PA. "Tell everyone that from now till closing, beer is one dollar!"

I said, "Uhhm what did you...

"FROM NOW til closing beer is a dollar!!" He interrupted.

So I stepped up to the mic and delivered the weird yet tender message.

Wow.

# PRAYER BALOONS

At a large youth event in Oklahoma, we were the house band for a week long conference. Each night different adults and youth would put the aspects of the worship service together.

On one of the night sessions, we had just finished our worship set, and the leader asked us to stay on the stage as the message was delivered. Afterwards they wanted us to play another song. The speaker had people distribute 1500 un-inflated balloons to the 1500 kids before his message (This wasn't a good idea if you were wondering.) He then instructed them to not blow up or play with the balloons yet. Yea right.

He wasn't 33 seconds into his talk when kids all over the auditorium started blowing up balloons, letting the air out, high pitched craziness abounded. It was hilarious and a frazzeled leader walked out to the mic and said, "DO NOT PLAY WITH YOUR BALOONS". Wayne-ology- lesson #105, - Never do this.

By the end of his talk, kids were antsy and there were glorious sounds of balloons squeeking. The speaker then asked everyone to "blow" their prayers into these balloons. After they had all done this, he said, "Now throw your prayers toward the stage and to God."

What?

There we were, just standing on the stage, me holding my guitar, as 1500 inflated balloons come floating towards us. My good friend and electric guitar player at the time, Rodney Black, began playing "Auld Lang Syne" which is the old time New

Year's Eve favorite. It was inappropriate but really funny .I quickly looked at him and gave him the international signal for "cut it out bro." Crazy. I felt sorry for whoever had to pick up and pop 1500 slobbery balloons from the stage that night.

# POWER SOURCE

In 2005, I did a CD called "Brand new day." I have usually tried to do a big CD release event whenever I have some new music coming out. This was my biggest undertaking so far. In faith, I rented the Merrell Center in Katy, Tx. We were estimating about 2000 kids coming based on ticket sales.

After months of working on the record and months on promoting the event, we were pumped to say the least about this event! The day of the concert, the sound company arrived from Austin. My man, Andy Davis, (Andy Audio) arrived to start setting up the massive light show.

The day was off to a good start, my band was arriving and volunteers were helping set up. There was a real sense of expectancy in the air.

Then we got the crazy news that there was a miscommunication between the facility people and the sound company. Long story short, they didn't have a "power feeder" to get power to the stage in the arena. Each side more or less blamed the other. It was a Sunday, and I knew it would be next to impossible to find this "power feeder" they were talking about.

It was 3 pm, and at 6:30 doors were opening to a few thousand youth. I could see the train wreck unfolding before my eyes. In my imagination I could see myself standing on the stage, yelling so everyone could hear me, making the lame announcement that the concert event couldn't happen because we forgot a huge extension cord.

Nice.

It was at that point that Rodney and I sat down and just decided to pray over the whole thing. Much of what had been done up to this point was done under our own power (pardon the pun). But clearly now we realized there was a spiritual battle going on over the night's event, and frankly, the enemy didn't want us telling a few thousand kids that Jesus Christ gives them a "Brand new day," and that He is crazy in love with them. Much of the theme of the CD is the newness of life that Jesus brings and wants for all of us to experience.

So we prayed.

We prayed that God would be glorified that night no matter what, even if there was no power.

We prayed that Jesus would be famous that night, and that I would not.

We prayed for peace in the midst of the craziness.

Shortly after, one of the event guys from the Merrell Center said he had been making some calls and somehow found a company open on a Sunday. They had the power feeder we needed. It was across town, but he was sending someone to pick it up.

The power cable arrived just in time. The doors opened and kids came streaming in. That night ended up being one of the most amazing events I've ever been a part of. The worship was unreal and authentic. I was reminded that day, that the real power does not come from within myself, my own dreams, desires or efforts. The true power comes when we submit our own will to that of our Heavenly Father. When we really give God the "steering wheel" of our lives, amazing things will happen. And I truly think, what He loves best, is walking through the adventure with us.

# PUPPET MINISTRY

Once when Rodney Black was playing with me, he did something weird at a concert we had in Lake Charles, Louisiana. We were 1/2 way into the concert and as I was doing a solo tune he disappeared behind the stage. I'm not sure if it was lack of sleep or too much time cramped in a rental vehicle, but something drove him over the edge that night. He reappeared from behind the choir area, but he wasn't alone. On his hand was a puppet he had found somewhere back there.

"Yikes," I thought. "Don't walk up to that microphone Rodney." Next thing you know, "Hi kids, meet my new friend "Sally"! He said out of the corner of his mouth.

"Sally?" Rodney, what are you doing?

The kids in the audience didn't know whether to laugh or boo, but Rod quickly began to crack everyone up, his ventrilliquism skills were not the best in the world, but he won the crowd.

"I can't see you guys, with these plastic eyes and all".

AMAZING!

We never really got the concert back on track that night. I laughed so hard I cried.

# PEACE CHAPEL

Lakeview is a United Methodist camp near Palestine, Tx. that holds a special place in my heart. Lakeview played a large role in the early days of my minstry. After I launched out in full-time ministry, that place became almost a second home. Summer camps, winter camps, it was amazing.

One of my favorite Lakeview moments took place in the small chapel building there called "Peace Chapel". It's a small old A-Frame style chapel which maybe seats 200 kids if you pack them in there. Wooden pews, high ceiling and the lighting fixtures looking like they were from 1962.

We were in there for an evening worship service during the middle of a summer camp. The place was packed full of high school students. I remember the night so vividly. We sang worship song after worship song and it honestly sounded like there were 1000 people in there singing it was so loud. By the time we reached the end of my set list of songs, every single person in there was still standing, and it seemed like no one wanted to move. I was in the front of the room at the piano, just playing softly as you could tell this was a powerful moment. The Bible says that "if two or more are gathered in His name, He is in the midst of them." Matt 18:20.

It seemed as if He had answered all our cries of worship! God always shows up! No one really knew what to do, but for sure... NO ONE wanted to leave.

I know this next part seems a bit strange, but bear with me. As I was playing, I almost audibly heard a voice whisper in my heart "Open up the mic." I thought, "Hmm... that's weird, must be my imagination."

Then again, "Open up the mic." As I continued to play the piano, I answered back in my head, "Well I didn't really clear that with anyone!"

"Open up the mic!" I heard one more time in my heart.

This time answering, "What if I do that, and no one comes up, I'll look like an idiot."

While I was having this back and forth argument with that "still small voice" in my head, I looked up and there was a young man standing before me at the piano. He leaned over and whispered in my ear, "Can I say something?"

Wow.

I said, "Yes please!" I had a shocked look on my face. I think the guy thought there was something seriously wrong with me. This high school senior took the mic, and began to share his heart, his testimony, his struggles, the way God was calling him back unto Christ!

It was a powerful experience. It was also a reminder to me that God does want to include us in His will, to use us. But if He needs to bypass us, and quit waiting on us, He will do that too.

# CROWD SURFING

The name says it all. I've thrown the caution to the wind a few times and hurled myself off the stage. It's pretty fun, providing they hold you up of course!

One time my good friend Charlie McAllister was directing one of his children's camps, and he saw me go off the stage into the audience during the final song. Emotions were high, everyone was jamming, kids were jumping like crazy people! All of this took Pastor Charlie's heart I think. He ran onto the stage and jumped out into the crowd.

Without going into detail, I'll let you figure out the rest. Let's just say it was a children's camp with 2nd through 5th graders. Pastor Charlie is 6"2 weighing in at a solid 230. AH, building memories in kids that will last.

And injuries?

IM KIDDING. Everyone was ok after the EMS folks arrived.

# TOO LOUD?

At a concert in Nebraska, I made a kid's ear bleed. Sorry again Vomacka family! I think if you make someone's ear bleed at one of your concerts, they should get free t-shirts, and free copies of EVERY CD that you have made, or EVER will make in your lifetime. That reminds me, I better mail him some stuff!

# TOMLIN

One time Chris Tomlin and I got double-booked accidently at the same church one Sunday morning in The Woodlands, Tx. I walked in carrying my gear and thought I heard someone sound checking. When I came through the doors, I saw Chris up on the stage. I thought, "Uh oh, either he is in the wrong place, or I am!" Come to find out, there was a slight scheduling misunderstanding, and we were both in the right place. They let him play that morning, probably a good call. I'm not bitter or anything.

# TRANSPOSE BUTTON

I once did a fund raising event with a few artists in Houston after Hurricane Katrina. It was amazing, we raised over $15,000 that night!

I did make a mistake that impacted one of my guests, Mr. Wayne Watson. Wayne is an amazing songwriter and very well known Grammy winning Christian artist. He donated his time that night, which was phenominal. He was up on stage right after us, and I did something pretty stupid. Sometimes when I am playing the keyboard, I transpose the piano down or up to another key, so that I can actually play the song in a key that is more familiar to me. It's like using a capo on a guitar and it lets you cheat a little.

WELL, our last song in the set was in a super weird key for me, so I hit the little transpose button, and had my piano 3 and 1/2 steps down from normal. I wanted to make sure not to forget to UNDO this button before Wayne Watson took the stage. I even left myself a post-it note on the keyboard so I would remember.

"Undo transpose button!"

We finished singing, I introduced him, my band and I walked off the stage and he began his first song at my keyboard. He was singing one of his famous songs, "Field of souls." I remember thinking, man something sounds weird, seems like he is singing a little low or something... "OH MY GOODNESS I forgot to UNDO that stupid transpose button!"

I remember grabbing Raymond Turner, amazing friend and drummer extraordinare, holding him by the shoulders, shaking him saying, "RAYMOND!!! I have the transpose on my keyboard and Wayne doesn't know!!! What do I do Raymond?!?!?!" "He has won a Grammy for pete's sake!!" Poor Rayray just looked at me in disbelief and shock.

A moment later, you could hear things change, as in fact Wayne saw the button, and put things back to normal.

Yikes.

The audience never knew or noticed, that guy is a real pro. He just rolled right on through. I think I apologized like 14 times to him. Here's #15. Sorry man! Mental note #132: leave a bigger post-it note.

# SPLASHTOWN

Splashtown is a pretty cool outdoor waterpark in the Houston area. One time we were playing a Christian event there with By the Tree and some others. The stage is directly in front of a giant wave pool. When we took the stage, I'd say there were over 1000 kids just floating in this wave pool right in front of us! Amazing sight to behold!    Fun.

I remember the excitement was in the air! We tore into the first tune, as my friend Brian Garcia would say... "Bringing the rock." or "Melting their faces with the goodness."

Immediately after the first song, the main lifeguard used the large PA to make a short announcement, "Everyone please exit the wavepool."

"What's up?" I asked him.
Off the mic he said, "Yep, every hour or so, we have to get everyone out just to give our lifeguards a break, but you guys can keep playing."

It was a glorious moment as we kept playing our hearts out, as hundreds upon hundreds of kids filed out right before our eyes. By the end of my 3rd song, there was not a single person in the wavepool! We just kept playing, looking out over a vast pool of empty water. Awesome.

# SOME RANDOM MOMENTS

• Once at a camp I accidently locked myself out of my room in the middle of the night after walking to the bathroom down the hall. I was in my boxers. Locked out. Not good.

• At a summer camp in Florida 2 guys doing a skit on stage slammed into my Taylor guitar and I saw it splinter into 7 pieces from the back of the room.

• In New Mexico, Micah Nicolaus and I tried to silence two high school guys on the basketball court. I splintered my ligaments in my ankle into about 7 pieces I think. AND... that night I asked Kelley to marry me with my ankle wrapped, elevated with an ice pack on it. I wore a blue boot for the next 6 weeks. *She said yes by the way!*

• At Second Baptist Beach Retreat (An amazing summer retreat), one of the ongoing daily skits involved the Youth Pastor coming on stage with a HUGE dead fish telling the kids it was alive. They would then let the fish do amazing feats like jumping thru a hoop and dancing, it was awesome.

BUT, one of the staffers who was co-leading worship there, told the Youth Pastor that the fish smelled HORRIBLE and to keep it away from his gear and specifically his microphone.

That night when the guys came out for the skit, they had the fish again. It was a little more decayed, and a little more smelly, and parts of it were flying off more and more as they would fling it around. The Youth Pastor took the fish and went straight for that worship leader's mic. With every exclamation point of his statements, he would hit the microphone with the fish... over and over, and over... It was hilarious and quite insane. That mic smelled bad all week long.

• I was leading a youth conference in Pennsylvania. A few students asked me to be involved in their skit they were doing on Saturday night. "Sure!" I said, "What do you guys have in mind?"

"OK," they said, "This one guy in our youth group is always showing up with no shirt on, and we want you to walk out on stage with him, and both of you guys should be shirtless while we make the announcements."

Uhhhhm.

"Let me think about it you guys~ ok NO!!!" I said, "A, I'd like to be invited back to this event again in the future, and B, I can see a photo of me on facebook appearing on the world wide web 30 seconds after I walk off the stage."

I don't think so.

• I played up in Arkansas with a fun and crazy youth minister guy I love named Mike Meeks. He has all the qualities it takes to be a successful youth pastor: fun, quite insane, and a deep love for Christ and for the kids he serves. I got to play up at his church last month, and the event was called BARF night. "Bring A Real Friend Night." He promised me there would be no projectile vomiting going on, but at youth events, you never know. They even printed a shirt for the event (which I have one by the way) that says, "BARF NIGHT, an evening with Wayne Kerr." I was assured this was NOT a subtle message in any way that my music will make one hurl their cookies.

• Prior to a Sunday night event at a church in Arkanasas, a man approached me and asked if he could bring his boys from a local half-way house to the concert. It was a home for guys 12-18 years old as an alternative to prison. He said they would be no problem at all, and they would come in and sit towards the back. He also said they have worship every day, and they'd love to join us. "Sure," we said. "Sounds awesome."

As the night started off, kids were having fun bouncing all around. There were a few hundred kids there. Several minutes into the night, I noticed the group of about 25 guys silently come into the back and sit on the very back rows. Most students up front didn't even notice them come in.

When we got towards the end of the night, I started playing some worship songs. I'll never forget the next thing I heard. Out of the back of the room you could hear a loud sound. It was the sound of 25 young men singing at the very top of their lungs. With no inhibitions at all, these guys were telling God of His faithfulness and how much they needed Him. Their singing was so loud in fact, that kids in the front were turning around almost wondering what was happening back there.

I was moved. I said, "I want to say thank you to the guys in the back of the room. Thank you for your heart to sing out to God. Some of us in this room know Jesus as a good guy, or the man who they talk about at church, but you guys sing like you know Him as Saviour and Redeemer. Once you have fallen off the boat into the stormy sea of life, you tend to be really thankful for the one who threw you a life preserver."

All of us were challenged by these great young men that night.

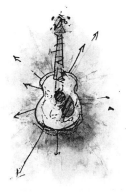

YES!! The perfect combination of fun times to be had. Snow, long road trips, bus loads of youth and tired adults. What could be better? AHaaaa.

For a few years in a row, it seemed every winter I was on a youth group ski trip somewhere. There were great bonding experiences for the groups, and some great worship times too. As you might imagine, I have a fun story or two to share here.

# SLOW ZONE

For the record I am no skier. My wife can snowboard and ski like nobody's business, granted she is from New Mexico. My excuse is that I am a native Houstonian, and it's beyond flat where I live. The nearest ski mountain is about 1000 miles away.

On one trip, I was trying to ski down the mountain with about 8 youth, but most of their time was spent waiting for me to catch up. Their lame ski run was made complete when I crashed into the "slow zone" sign.

Ah yes, nothing says "cool musician" like being tangled in an orange mesh sign in the area where little kids take ski lessons. My skis and poles had gone everywhere. I on the other hand was clearly going nowhere, being tangled in this big orange sign. They all got out their cameras and took pics of me for the world to see.

# BRUTAL ROAD TRIP

By far the ski experience that sticks out the most in my mind involves bus travel. I was scheduled to co-lead some worship with my friend (and now pastor) Matt Neely. The trip started out on a late Saturday night, but since Matt and I were both already booked at local churches for Sunday we couldn't leave with the group. They agreed to fly us to the halfway point. We would fly to Amarillo, Tx. and meet up with the two buses as they made their way onto Colorado. Then once the trip was over, we would do the full twenty two hour trip back to Houston on the bus.

On Sunday, and Matt and I met at the airport and boarded our plane. It was a short hour and a half to Amarillo. We took a shuttle to a local motel there. We weren't checking into the hotel to stay over, it was just the drop off location for the bus drivers to switch drivers. We were supposed to wait there for about an hour for the buses to come through.

At the motel, we made ourselves comfy in the lobby. 8pm came, 9pm, 10pm. We asked the the lady working behind the registration desk if she had heard anything from the bus companies. She said that one of the buses wouldn't start properly in Houston, and they had to actually wait for another bus. Yikes. She assured us it would only be a slight delay.

11pm turned into midnight. Midnight turned into 1am. There's only so much you can do sitting in a chair in a motel lobby that looks (and smells) like it is still 1970. We asked again if there was any info, she said the buses would arrive at any time. 2am. 3am.

At 4am, the buses pulled into snowy Amarillo. If we would have known it would have been so late, I guess he and I could have booked a room and at least rested. At this point, Matt and I had been awake for 22 hours straight, and the last 9 hours we were sitting and pacing in a motel lobby.

We boarded the buses in the darkness, both of us looked like we had been run over by a bus. The kids were asleep all spread out over the bus. Somehow in the darkness I found an empty seat, and I covered up with my jacket. I fell asleep instantly. Three and a half hours later I was awakened by all the kids talking and laughing, and the morning sun was coming thru the windows. As my blurry vision was brought into focus by putting on my glasses, I was aware that there were about 8 kids standing over me, most likely watching me drool all over my ski coat. I'm sure most of them were thinking, "This is the music guy? He looked way cooler on the poster! He looks pretty rough!"

I tried to be Jesus with skin on to the kids, and not let my grumpiness come through, but it was difficult. A girl behind me was getting her over stuffed backpack down from the storage area above and it dropped right on my head.

Yes.   Building memories.

We finally arrived at the ski area, and our week was underway. Everything went great during the trip. One token broken arm, one case of altitude sickness, and two or three dehydration headaches. Other than that, no major issues. The worship times went great, other than the one night they asked us to have our session outside. Yes, it was only 18 degrees.

Then came time for our bus ride all the way back to Houston. I had just nearly recovered from our trip there when it was time to head back. The first 10 hours were smooth.

At 2 am I woke up after hearing a weird sound. The sound I was hearing was ice breaking off the windshield of the bus. We were working our way through a pretty rough snow and ice storm. The sounds made by large windshield wipers going over ever increasingly icey windows is pretty scary when you are going 70 mph down a snowy highway. Visibility was getting worse and worse, and to be honest, I was starting to freak out.

I could hear the driver talking with a dispatch person as they were trying to figure out what to do. Basically they were being told of a massive winter storm that was closing highways up ahead. We pulled into a small town and unloaded at a hotel. I was beyond thrilled that we were off the highway. I was less than thrilled when they told us that there were no rooms available to rent out. The bus driver said, "We can't keep going on those roads." The Best Western was gracious enough to help us out. There were no rooms available, but they let all 45 of us go into a large meeting room they had open. This was now our "bedroom" for the night. 45 youth, 10 adults, and two worship leaders all sleeping on the floor in a big empty room. The snow and ice storm raged on outside.

I remember laying on my back flat on the cold hard floor looking up at the ceiling thinking, "This is the most insane trip I have ever been on in my entire existence."

Since that trip, I've accepted bookings for a ski trip or two, but I flew. I have officially waved-off cross country bus trips.

# 2 THINGS I'VE LEARNED FROM STEVEN CURTIS CHAPMAN

Though we have not met, God has used him two different times to speak a word right to my heart.

**1.)** I was @ Youth Specialties in San Diego. Ahhhhh... great area. If you ever get a chance to visit there you've got to do it! Go to the zoo "fo sho". Ok sorry, I'm rambling.

One of the nights Youth Specialties had several great artists, all pretty popular in the day, I won't mention the names, but you would know who they are. The headliner that night was Steven Curtis Chapman. You could hear the chatter of many youth workers that day, "I cant wait to see this band, or that band," "Steven Curtis Chapman is kinda old school though." I heard one of them say. Many of them were more excited to see the newest and coolest bands. That night, one band got up and talked and talked about their new album that was out. The next band talked and talked about their new tour upcoming. Steven was last, and guess what? He ministered to those there. Novel thought eh?

He said, "I'm so thankful for what you folks do, you all are in the real trenches of ministry. You are loving kids. And if it weren't for a youth pastor who reached out to me when I was young, I don't know where I would be today." He then said, "This time is for you guys... to reconnect to HIM, to be reminded of your first love, and to drink from the well that will empower you to love these kids." Over 3000 youth pastors were engaged in an amazing time of worship. I remember seeing hands raised all over the room, tears flowing down, healing taking place. I feel as if God tapped me on the forhead and said, "Wayne, lesson #132, if I ever place you in front of any audience, remember it is a chance to minister to them and to encourage them, it is NOT a chance to sell the new thing you are trying to peddle.

That night made a big impact on me.

**2.)** Several years later, I was in Nashville for the GMA (Gospel Music Association) week. While I was in an elevator going up, it stopped on the 3rd floor and in walked Steven Curtis Chapman and a few folks who were on his management team. As we were riding up, I just stood there... like really what was I gonna say, "Dude you're famous!" Or, "Hey, do you know who you are?" So i opted for saying nothing. His manager said "Hey Steven we got those photos back." "Oh cool." he said. They started looking through them, and naturally I leaned over to see what was up! During this time, he had taken a couple years off from touring, recording and performing to spend time with his boys who were growing up before his eyes. I had read an article that he had done 15 years straight with no break. (Kinda reminds me of myself at this point— minus the famous part.)

SO back to the elevator... I leaned over, and saw that it was pictures from some recent prison ministry he had been involved with. Here is a guy who has done amazingly well in the Christian music industry, and even in a season of taking a break from touring, he was investing in God's people. In that moment God showed me that Steven was actually in the "ministry." This whole thing wasn't just a "gig" to him. He is authentic and the real deal. Even when he was not out touring big shows, he was in ministry. The doors opened and off they went.

It was God lesson #133 for me. Steven is a guy who fully understands it's not all about him. God can use us if we are simply vessels for Him to pour through.

# CAMPS

I can't say enough about getting students away for a summer camp, mission trip, a weekend getaway. I see real impact on lives. God does amazing things when people get out of their normal day-to-day surroundings, and go to a place where He can speak to them.

All through scripture, you see the people of God taking time to go away and be with the Father. They go to pray, they go to be refueled, and they go for comfort in time of need.

Exodus 19:20
[Moses] The Lord descended to the top of Mount Sinai and called Moses to the top of the mountain.

Matthew 15:29
[Jesus feeds the four thousand] Jesus left there and went along the Sea of Galilee. Then He went up on a mountainside and sat down.

Mark 1:35
[Jesus prays alone] Very early in the morning, while it was still

dark, Jesus got up, left the house and went off to a solitary place, where He prayed.

Luke 9:28
[Jesus] took Peter, John and James with Him and went up onto a mountain to pray.

Matthew 14:23
[Jesus] After He dismissed them, He went up on a mountainside by Himself to pray. When evening came, He was there alone.

Time and time again we see this. Seriously, if it's good enough for Jesus, it's good enough for me. We NEED time to go away and reconnect to the vine. Jesus said, "I am the true vine, you are the branches. If a man remains in me and I in him, he will bear much fruit; apart from me he can do nothing." John 15:5

I do know that God inhabits the praise of His people. Even the kid with the hardest heart cannot withstand the love assault that is placed on him from Christ. I truly believe anyone who retreats for as little as 2 1/2 days and is surrounded by worshippers, God's Word, and love from a community of believers, will undergo a heart change. Just the freedom to actually act like a kid and have fun at some of these retreats is beyond life giving.

If you are a youth,  please go on a fall or winter retreat with a youth group.  Please go to a summer camp.  Please go and serve on a mission trip for a week. Some of the most beautiful moments I've seen were of students on a mission trip, who went to give to others, and in the end received so much instead.

If you are an adult, please consider volunteering on a fall or winter retreat with a youth group. Please consider taking a week of your vacation during summer to invest into the next generation. I promise, you'll be blessed beyond your wildest imagination. And adults... ya'll are amazing! Camps and retreats don't happen without you. If you've ever considered going, do it! You won't regret it, just ask my friend, Roni Allen.

# YOU'VE BEEN CUT

Several years ago I was given a great opportunity to play at the Texas Baptist Youth Conclave. My band and I were there to support a great worship leader, Stephen Smith, in leading the music that week. There were to be about 3000 Baptist youth Pastors there! Pretty amazing opportunity for sure. Stephen and his wife, Star, are incredible worship leaders, and we were blessed to be there with them and help out musically. Stephen told me that on one of the nights a young aspiring artist would be given the stage to share her ministry, and do one song. Since he knew I was in full-time ministry, he wanted to give me the same opportunity.

My mind began to race as to which song I would do, and how I would introduce myself. What would I say in that crucial 30 seconds? Could this open new and amazing opportunities? Camps? Gigs? In hind sight I so clearly see the error of my ways. The thoughts going through my mind where not, "Which song might encourage these Youth Pastors to keep going?" "Which song will create an atmosphere of worship so these leaders will be reminded of Christ and all He has done."

Instead I was thinking of myself. 2 weeks before Conclave I worked tirelessly on a tri-fold brochure that would be placed at the back of the arena. I felt that these Youth Pastors would need a way to contact me after my performance. I printed up 500 of them.

During Conclave, the sessions were going great. Stephen was doing an amazing job, things were off to a smooth start. In fact there were more than 3000 folks there. Night #2 meant the young artist from Stephens' church was to have her spot. She shared her heart, a few words about her ministry, then she sang her song. She nailed it, and was the buzz all the next day.

All that day I kept going back and forth between which song I'd perform, again with the wrong motive at the forefront. By the time the night session came along, I was ready to go. That night the artist Tait from DC talk was there and he did the opening set. He went just a little long. Then a few skit folks took the stage and they went just a tad long. Next I went up with Stephen and Star to lead worship, to be followed by my tune. The worship set went well, but my mind was distracted by what was coming next... my little "moment in the spotlight".

As the last worship song wrapped up, Stephen walked back to us as I was getting ready and said they had told him via his ear monitor that we were running late on time. My song needed to be cut. I couldn't believe it.

We walked off the stage, and I was at a loss for words. My band guys were mad for me, because they could see the disappointment on my face. I stood behind the stage as the speaker took the stage. Dave Edwards. An amazing guy who I've known for years. All that was going through my mind was, "Why did they let that girl share her song, and I got cut?" I looked up at the projection screen and heard Dave declare, "Tonight I'm going to talk about the sin of comparison!"

The Holy Spirit so clearly, I mean CLEARLY broke me down that night! Dave shared how we get caught up in "my ministry vs. their ministry" mindset, when we are all on the same team. We should be Kingdom minded. I was in extreme error at this event. What was I thinking? Instead of focusing on worship, I was focused on self-promotion.

I remember a moment when Dave asked everyone to close their eyes for prayer, and then for anyone who was dealing with comparison in their lives to hold up their hand. I stood behind the stage all alone, with my hand in the air, as Dave prayed for all of us. It was good to come clean with God!

The next morning, they did give me a chance to sing my tune. Since it was the closing session, there were about 1/5th of the people there. Most of the pastors already left. As Conclave concluded, I remember being at the back table and loading all 500 brochures back into the box they came in. It was a humbling moment. I asked God to forgive my selfishness. Doesn't this story sound familiar?

I'm so thankful for times in my life when God reveals Himself. When I let God do all the work, things turn out better. Like once I went to a small town in Missouri to do an event in Chillicothe. With no thought of self promotion, I was just excited to be there. That night an amazing lady, Beverly Boehmer, walked up to me and said, "I work on this big event here in Missouri with thousands of youth, you and your band should be at this." God opened an amazing opportunity when I wasn't looking to promote myself.

This much I know, I was not created to bring Glory to myself. I was created to bring Glory to HIM. When we try to grab some glory, fame, attention or accolades, it's almost like trying to hold a cloud. We simply cannot do such a thing, we are not capable.

I have resolved then to the best of my ability to not compare myself to anyone. It's so freeing. I can simply be who God has created me to be! I can let them be them. On top of that, I don't have to try and get people to like me or like the music I put out there. I fall back into comparison sometimes. I think creative people always wear their heart on their sleeve a little bit.

However, I know that I know we are simply created to bring HIM glory!

# AMAZING GOD

I received a powerful note via facebook. I wanted to include this here, not to in any way to bring glory to me, but to show how good God is, and how faithful He is to use us to share His love in this world. I sent this young lady a note today and asked if I could include this letter in my book, she agreed to let me.

*Dear Wayne,*
*-I was confirmed my 6th grade year and you were at my confirma-*
*tion camp. I drew you a picture and you told everybody I think the*
*last day of camp but I never gave you my name. Well I bought your*
*cd and it was my favorite for the longest time. Then towards the*
*end of high school I lost my faith with God because I was going*
*through a really rough time with my family and I put your cd away*
*for a few years. But I recently found it when I moved away to col-*

lege and I started to listen to it again. Now that Im a sophomore at college, it made me realize that God lets us go through hard times cause it makes us stronger and he wouldn't do something to us that he knows we cant handle. My boyfriend recently lost his little brother but through listening to your music and really getting back into my faith both of us are going to church every sunday night and it is really helping him a lot. So I wanted to thank you so much for your music. you probably get these kind of letters all the time but I really wanted to thank you for it.
Never stop singing.

Ashley

# SKYYE

Yep, 2 y's and and e tossed in there at the end, just to be cute, I guess. Skyye arrived on the scene after Kelley and I got married. A new home, a new life together for us, and our new dog! Ahhh great times. This guy was like Houdini. For those of you who are too young to know who the heck that is, he was a super famous escape artist back in the day. He was known for getting out of straight jackets while underwater, while in a tank, while being lifted over niagra falls... yep, that kinda guy. Skyye was a beautiful Siberian Husky that we rescued from the Houston Humane Society. From day one, he was part of the family.

One day I took Skyye out for a fun "man and his dog" kinda day. We went to a huge park in the Houston area called "Bear Creek Park." This place is really enormous. It is over 7,600 acres and in the spring it is beautiful. On this particular day, it was perfect... blue skies... 75 degrees.

Like most huskies, Skyye would sometimes run off if he got a whiff of some animal or heard something in the trees, so most of the time we kept this guy on a leash. We loved to play this game where I would briefly take him off the leash, tell him to sit, and slowly walk away. "Stay"... "Stay," I would say as I got further and further away. Then I would finally yell, "COME ON!" I would start running like a crazy man away from him while he would sprint after me. In no time flat, my slightly out of shape 2 legged self would be overcome by his lean and mean 4 legged Siberian self. Then we would jump around and be goofy. Like I said, "a man and his dog" kinda day.

After 4 or 5 of these sprint / run / tackle exercises, I felt it was time to test his "stay-ability." In a big open area in the park, I took him off his uber-red leash. "Sit." "Good boy." "Stay." I walked away. "Stay." 15 feet, 20 feet, "Stay....good boy." 30 feet, 50 feet. It was at about this time that something in the nearby trees could be heard shuffling around. His head spun. "Stay," I said firmly. Then his bionic super dog nose caught a trace of something that made his instincts kick in. He bolted. Not towards me this time, but straight into the woods.

"SKYYE!!!" "NO!!"

Off he went, like a shot! "SKYYYYEEE!" "Come here boy." I tried my trick of running the opposite way, hoping he would change his mind and instead run after me! Nope. Into the woods he went. I sprinted back over to where he was, shouting his name the entire time. As I reached the edge of the trees I could faintly hear him barking, no doubt chasing a bird, or a deer, or who knows what.

I shouted his name over and over, all the while standing on the edge of this forest. "Well," I thought. "Into the woods I go." I started working my way into the thicket, trying to peer through the trees to keep an eye out for his white and black puffy tail. I couldn't see him anywhere, or for that matter, hear him any longer either. It was muddy back in there and my thoughts went to my brand new New Balance shoes I was wearing.

I worked my way back out into the clearing, thinking maybe he had come full circle and came back to where we were before. No luck. No sign of him anywhere. It was at this point that I started to actually get worried about the situation. The first thoughts of really losing my dog came across my mind. I would do anything in my power to not let that happen.

Off into the woods I ran, this time not at all thinking of my stupid shoes, or the thorns and bushes that were cutting my legs and arms. I began running at a full sprint thru the trees shouting his name.

"SKYYE!"  "SKYYYYEE!!!!"

It was in those moments that I had an amazing God encounter.

As I ran through the trees, doing whatever it took to find him, I felt as if the Lord brought my mind to the story of the lost sheep. In Matt. 18:12-14, Jesus tells the story of a man who had a hundred sheep, and one of them wandered off. Sounded familiar. "Will he not leave the ninety-nine on the hills, and go to look for the one that wandered off? And if he finds it, he is happier about that one sheep than about the ninety-nine that did not wander off. In the same way, our Father in heaven, is not willing that any of His little ones should be lost."

I felt an amazing new understanding of what Christ did to find me when I was lost. I almost could hear Him say.... "I would do WHATEVER it takes to find you and bring you home, Wayne." As I ran through bushes and thorns, I could hear Him saying, "I was scarred and bruised for you Wayne!" As even my legs and arms were bleeding, I could hear Him say softly... "I bled for you Wayne." I stopped right in my tracks, tears streaming down my face. Though I felt sad that I may have lost my awesome dog that day, I felt an amazing peace over me. That kind of feeling which I can't describe,  a deep sense that God Himself had whispered to me.

I walked back to my truck, and drove to the front ranger station of the park.  They looked a little alarmed when I walked in. Sweat soaked shirt, mud all over, and arms and legs (and face) slightly cut up. After telling them of the situation with my dog, they radioed the other rangers to keep a look out for him. One last time I drove all around the park, all the while remembering the sacrifice Jesus made for me to ensure that I wouldn't be lost.

Four hours had now gone by, and the sun was beginning to set. After all this time of running through the woods, I was officially ready to pack it in.  I made one last stop by the ranger station on the way out. One of the park workers said, "Someone just radioed in a few minutes ago and they said they saw someone in a car pull up. A black and white dog got in with them.  They drove away before we could catch up to them."

That was it.  Skyye was gone.

I told the rangers thanks anyway, and I left. I called Kelley to tell her the news of losing our dog. It was a pretty sad time to be honest. Just then my cell phone rang, and there was a guy on the other end saying, "I think I found your dog!" Someone was actually honest enough to call the number on his tag and return our dog to us! "He's looking pretty disheveled and pretty muddy, so I'm gonna give him a bath, then we can meet up." Wow. I was so thankful. Again my mind raced to the scripture God had reminded me of. The joy the Father must feel when one that is lost is truly found. Im not talking a guy losing his dog kind of joy, Im talking the Creator knowing what He had created is returning home!

I met up with Emilio at a corner gas-station. There was my dog, who ironically looked like he only weighs 20 pounds when he's wet! I loaded up Skyye, and thanked Emilio for his honesty, and for calling. I told him I didn't have much to give, but wanted to give him a copy of my new CD. "It's Christian music." I said, "And I hope it'll bless you in some small way."

"Whoa," He said with a fairly shocked look on his face. "I'm not sure what's going on, but all this week there have been all these crazy things happening telling me to go back to church, now I find a lost dog of some guy who is a Christian singer... I better go back to church."

I'm not sure what all God was up to that day, in Emilio's heart or mine, but I'm thankful for it. We all feel a little lost sometimes.

Do you need to run home today?

He's waiting.

START

END

Marathon
story

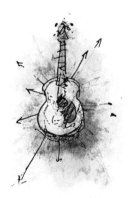

"Therefore, since we are surrounded by such a great cloud of witnesses, let us throw off everything that hinders and the sin that so easily entangles, and let us run with perseverance the race marked out for us." Hebrews 12:1

A few years ago, Kelley came home and said, "I think I may be inspired to run a marathon." She explained how a good friend of hers at church had run the Houston marathon, and just loved it. Susan had inspired her! She said, "I'm thinking about signing up for the Houston marathon coming up, well I sorta, well, ok I already signed up for it."

"Whoa, whoa... back up." I said. "You already signed up?"

"Yep," she said with that cute smile of hers.

At that point I asked the question that I thought should be asked. "Honey, Do you run? I've never seen you out running or anything! How far is a marathon anyway?"

For all of you running and/or history buffs who know the origin of the marathon, you skip the following paragraph. For those of you who were like me and had no clue, please read on.

The name Marathon comes from the Greek legend of a guy named Pheidippides, how you pronounce that, I have no clue. Let's call him Phil for the sake of our story. Phil was in a major battle in a city named Marathon in 490 BC. He was sent from the battlefield to Athens to bring good news of the war. It is said that he ran the entire way to Athens without stopping. He ran a total distance of approx 26.2 miles, around a mountain no less. He burst into the assembly and exlcaimed, "We have won!" Then he collapsed and died.

The part that gets me is that there was some greek guy standing there and thought, "Hey this will make a great sport!" Yikes!

26.2 miles. That's a long way I thought for a beautiful young woman like my wife to run. If I were to be honest with you, and I'm sad to say, I had my doubts if she could do it. She explained about an organization called Katy Fit. She would train with this team over a 5 month period.

Week #1 she went 3 miles. Week #2 she went 4 miles. Week #3 she went 5 miles. I was watching this before my eyes, and though still skeptical, I was beginning to see she was determined.

Once the training reached 8 miles, I thought "Ok enough of me on the sidelines here, I need to do a better job of supporting and encouraging my baby!!!!" (Slang marriage talk.) So the morning of her early departure to go run 8 miles, I woke up before her and drew on a piece of paper a "You can do it" sign. I drew a really big 8 on it, and wrote underneath, "GO KELLEY, YOU CAN DO IT!" I then stuck the drawing on the bathroom mirror for her to see when she woke up at 5:30 am. "Awweee..." go ahead and say it. I know, I'm a cheeseball.

Week after week, I watched her stick to her regiment. Through good weather, bad weather, sunny mornings, rainy cold mornings, she ran. 8 miles turned into 10 miles. 10 miles turned into 12 miles. 12 miles turned into 15 miles. Amazing.

Now pause the story right here, and let me interject a sub-plot to this lovely narrative. Let me direct this paragraph to all the married guys out there, or at least any guy with a girlfriend. Ok, any guy who will grow up to have either. When your wife is in WAY better shape than you, it starts to mess with the male psyche. I mean let's be real here, she is out running 15 miles like it's nothing, and I need an oxygen tank to get to my mailbox? Not good.

I decided, it was time for me to get in the game here. Time for Wayne-o to dust off the running shoes and get out there. I quickly realized how out of shape I was. But after a week or two I started feeling pretty good about myself! Where we live there is a big loop that goes around the neighborhood, and we figured out that it's about 1/2 mile around. After much training I reached the point where I could go... hold your applause... drum roll please... I could go- 2 loops without stopping!! 1 MILE! The crowd goes wild! I know, I know, pretty sad in comparison.

This became painfully apparent one morning when she came home from a long Saturday morning run (12 miles) and stuck her head in the house and said, "Just wanted to let you know I am home! I'm gonna go do 2 loops as a cool down." That's right sports fans, my "workout" is my wifes "cooldown". YIKES.

OK, back to the story. Kelley kept up her training. 3 months in, 4 months in... 17 miles, 18 miles. At this point, our bathroom mirror was covered with numbers and papers and "you can do it" notes. Then came time for her last long run before the actual marathon. 22 miles. The Katy Fit leaders basically told her, "If you can run 22 miles, you'll be physically able to run the full 26.2 in 3 weeks. It just depends on if you are mentally up for it."

22 miles is a long way. It's a long way to drive. My dad would most likely want to get his oil changed before making such a long trip! Kelley left that morning as usual at 5 am to meet up with her team. According to her pace, this run should take her

about 4 hours. At around 9am, I started looking at my watch wondering when I would hear from her. 9:30 there was still no news or call on my cell phone. Just then my phone rang and it was her. All she said was, "Turn... bath... water... on!!"

"Are you ok?" I asked. She was good, just suuuuuper tired!

When she walked in the door, I remember seeing these small white lines on her forehead, and around her neck. Salt.

WOW! I was so proud of her. I was in the process of formulating my plans of how be a her #1 cheerleader as she ran the race coming up. I had it all planned out. I made a series of big giant signs on poster boards stapled to pieces of wood. One said, "GO KELLEY." One said "GO BABY GO!" I had printed out the race route, and had it all mapped out. Basically, I planned to meet up with her at about 5 locations along the run, actually jump in with her, and run for a few seconds. I would have a backpack with me of various things she may or may not need. Orange slices, protein bars, these weird carb and energy goo packets that runners use.

Race day had arrived. It was on January 17th on a Sunday morning. That day the temperature at sunrise was 35 degrees. It was amazingly cold, and somewhat unusual for the Houston area.

The Houston Marathon is a pretty huge event. Over 17,000 runners take on the half and full marathons. Over 200,000 people come out and line the streets to support the runners, it's a pretty incredible thing to see.

BANG!! A cannon went off in the early morning chill, and the race had begun. I heard a huge cheer from the thousands of excited runners! This thing was off and running... pardon the pun.

I had my map in hand, backpack ready, and truck gassed up. The first stop to meet up with Kelley was at about the 5 mile mark in the race, near the Heights area of Houston. My parents lived in that area at the time and they wanted to be part of my first stop. I picked them up and headed to my location.

When we arrived there, you could hear the cheers like crazy. Many of the roads were closed off due to the run, and the excitement was in the air. We parked and worked our way through the onlookers. When we got to the street, hundreds, thousands of runners were pouring by in this giant mass, almost like one living organism. So many people! At that point it hit me, "How was I thinking I could just show up and see Kelley in the midst of all these people?" I recruited my mom and dad, and told them to help me look for Kelley. "She's wearing a black shirt, and her hair is pulled back, like every other girl out here." Eeeesh. I looked at my watch, according to her pace, at any moment we should see them. There we were, mom, dad and I standing shivering in the cold with our coats on. I was proudly holding my big sign that said, "GO BABY GO."

Just then, we spotted Kelley and her two running mates. "There they are!" I shouted. I threw the sign to my dad, and jumped into the race with her. "How are you doing?" I asked as we ran along. "GREAT" she said, smiling from ear to ear. I could not have been more proud of my wife for what she was doing. I made it about 100 yards and then realized I was out of breath. "OK." I said, panting. "Keeeeep going!!! I'll meet you at the next point!"

I ran back to get my parents, and found my dad still standing there holding up the sign, "GO BABY GO." He said, "I might as well cheer on all these people!"

After I quickly got my parents back home, I headed off to meet her at location #2. This was at approximately mile #12. She was still doing great. I met up with her again at mile #17 near the Galleria area in Houston. "You can do it!" I told her as she ran off.

The last time we met up before the finish line was at mile #22 or so. At this point she was 4 hours into the race, and still pressing on. I parked my truck and walked down toward the street to meet up with them. At this point in the marathon, people were much more spread out. The faster runners had already finished, gone home and had coffee. But the majority of the "regular" humans were still in the process of the race.

I stood there looking for Kelley and her two running mates. There was no sign of them yet. I looked again at my watch, and felt at any minute I should see them coming over the hill. Just then I saw them! Kelley and her two co-runners she had been training with were still crankin' along. I jumped in to run with them. This time things were not going as smoothly. One of the girls running with her was fighting a calf cramp. With every step she took there was massive pain, but she was trying to press through. It showed on her face that this was not good. The other girl running with Kelley was having a toe cramp. I don't even know what a toe cramp is, but I never want one. With every step, she too was pretty miserable.

Kelley on the other hand was doing amazingly well. "That step I took is the furthest I've ever run!!!" She shouted with a huge smile on her face. "That step I took is the furthest I've ever run!!!" She was pumped. I remember thinking, "Hey don't look too happy, cuz toe cramp girl looks like she's ready to punch somebody!"

I passed along my last remaining energy goo and orange slice and said farewell. "I'll meet you at the end. YOU CAN DO IT!!!"

As I headed back to my truck, I felt a little worried about Kelley and the girls being able to make it to the end. Here's the bad thing- The Houston marathon is basically a flat race. If you were to look at a map you'd see its pretty much level going most of the way, except for the last 4 miles. There's a street in Houston called Allen Parkway that winds it's way into downtown. Up and down it goes. It's very hilly. I was fearful for Kel and her friends. I drove into downtown, trying to navigate all the closed streets. I've lived in Houston my whole life, but I was astounded at how clueless I seemed to be at getting around town. With all the street closures, I was having some serious issues. I thought this would be SO LAME if I saw Kelley all along the way, but missed seeing her cross the finish line. Finally, I found a place to park, and ran as quick as I could to get down to the finish.

There were thousands of people gathered at the finish line. You could hear the cheers from blocks away. I worked my way through the crowds, and finally got to where I could see the finish line. There was a giant blue overpass that covered the finish line. As runners would cross the line, an announcement would go out over the sound system... "64228, Hillary Johnson," and people would cheer like crazy. Each and every runner would be called out as they crossed the finish line, it was pretty amazing to witness.

I was hoping I wasn't too late. I knew Kelley's goal was to finish the marathon in under 5 hours. I looked up through the fencing and saw the huge clock, it said 4:58. Just then I turned, looked, and saw her coming down the street, still running. This time the other 2 girls were no longer with her. Just like that, she crossed the line. "45119, Kelley Kerr!"

At that point it was very surreal. It was almost like in those old movies when there was a "dream sequence." I stood there watching her cross the line, and it was almost in slow motion. The sounds of the crowds faded away, and all became silent.

It was at this moment that I had an amazing God encounter. In a way it's hard to describe, but I almost audibly heard Gods' voice in my heart say, "Do you see how excited you were for her in her race? How much more am I excited for you in your race of life?"

"Do you see how excited you were for her in her race? How much more am I excited for you in your race of life?"

"Whoa, that was weird." The sound of the crowds came back, the screaming, the runners crossing the line, the announcer. I shook it off and went to go find Kelley. I saw her and ran up and hugged her. I was so amazed at what she had accomplished.

To put into perspective how much of an amazing woman I am married to, the night of the marathon(Sunday) Kelley had youth group to lead at the church. At like 5pm the night of the race, she was getting ready to go lead 220 Jr .Highers. Meanwhile I was on the couch exhausted from the long day. I wish I was making this up, but I'm not. As she was leaving the house, she turned to me... sprawled out on the sofa, and asked, "Can I get you anything?" "I want a root beer," I said in a pitiful voice. "I feel like I just ran a marathon." Wow, did I really say that? Yes.

That night, and over the next couple days, that still small voice kept reverberating in my heart. "Did you see how excited you were for her in her race? How much more am I excited for you in your race of life?"

I began to think about how incredibly excited I was to watch Kelley run the long race. I began to think about the God of the universe actually being excited for you and me as we walk through this life. Could God honestly care one way or another about the directions our lives take? Does He celebrate when we make decisions that honor Him? Does the heart of God break when we turn our backs on Him?

IS GOD EXCITED ABOUT YOUR LIFE TODAY??

The bible gives me some insight into this:

God rejoices in you and even sings over you.
Zephaniah 3:17

You were made in God's image.
Genesis 1:27

God is familiar with all your ways.
Psalm 139:3

Even the very hairs on your head are numbered.
Matthew 10:29-31

God knew you even before you were even born.

Jeremiah 1:4-5

He chose you when He planned creation.
Ephesians 1:11-12

You were not a mistake, all your days are written in His book.
Psalm 139:15-16

You are fearfully and wonderfully made.
Psalm 139:14

God wants to give you a hope and a future.
Jeremiah 29:11

He loves you with an everlasting and amazing love.
Jeremiah 31:3

God's thoughts toward you are countless as the sand on the seashore.  Psalm 139:17-18

Delight in Him and He will give you the desires of your heart.
Psalm 37:4

God comforts you in all your troubles.
2 Corinthians 1:3-4

God will wipe away every tear from your eyes.
Revelation 21:3-4

In Jesus, God's love for you is revealed.
John 17:26

God is not counting your sins.

2 Corinthians 5:18-19

God has an amazing party planned for you.
Luke 15:7

God declares that you are His child.
John 1:12-13

Wow.

God is clearly cheering for you and me today.

During the weeks and months that came after Kelley's
marathon, the still small voice of God continued to stir in my
heart. I felt as if there were SO MANY life lessons in this for me.
I recognized the amazing truth that our walk with God is more
like a marathon than a sprint. God is more interested in being
involved in your race over your entire lifetime , not just part of
the time.

If you are feeling like your run hasn't been going too well, I pray
you'll take encouragement in this story. Don't give up! Maybe
your toe is cramping, maybe your calf is cramping and you want
to give up on God. Don't do it. The scriptures I've pointed to
show that He is for you and will never leave or forsake you!

Kelley told me about one girl who had done the training in
Katy. During the race, she was distracted and took a wrong turn
at the 1/2 marathon turn off. She was several miles down the
path when she realized her error. She didn't have the opportunity to finish the full marathon. Kelley saw her afterwards and
the young lady was obviously upset. Can you imagine? 5 months
of your life devoted to training for an event, with one wrong

decision it was all over.

THANK GOD that He does not treat us in this way.

Read this story:
Luke 15:11-32

At different times during the race when I would jump in with Kelley, we would come around a corner and there would be such unexpected blessings. Along the route there were live bands out there playing, at one point there was a 35 foot inflated godzilla, we even came across 13 Elvis impersonators who were singing "viva keep running".   Crazy.

If you are feeling down, or beating yourself up from something you did today, or last week, or 4 months ago, or 4 years ago, receive the forgiveness He wants you to have!  The bible says the old is gone and the new has come.  Jesus brings you newness of life! Right around the corner there may be a huge blessing, don't give up!

I pray you know today that God is in fact excited for you in your face of life. And when you say "YES" to Jesus Christ in your life, you basically put on "HIS" number. And in that moment, I believe in heaven, God says "YES!" and He is beyond excited to be with you in your race of life! He is for you. The God I've come to know doesn't say, "Hey good luck with that life thing, I'm really busy, I'm sure you'll do great. I'll just meet you at the end, and Ill cheer for you as you cross the line."  No.

The God I know says, "I will indeed be with you, I am for you and I love you. In fact, I won't just meet you at the end of the race, I will run with you and I have a backpack with me filled with all you will ever need."

"Therefore, since we are surrounded by such a great cloud of witnesses, let us throw off everything that hinders and the sin that so easily entangles, and let us run with perseverance the race marked out for us." Hebrews 12:1

ah...
camping

My wife and I got married in 2001. I'm so blessed to be married to an amazing Proverbs 31 woman. You guys out there, read that chapter in the Bible, and then keep your eyes and ears pealed for a girl like that.

We bought about 20 acres of land south of Schulenburg, Tx. We decided to go tent camping on our 8th anniversary. Out on our property there's really not much there. No cabin, no electricity, no water. There is only God's beautiful creation and the out-door table and 4 chairs we have left out there.

Our neighbors out there had told us recently to be careful of the wild hogs out there. In fact, they had shot a 300 pound hog on our property a few months ago.

We weren't too concerned about it, and made our plans to camp out. We had all the basic needs covered: tent, firewood, air mat-tress (I can't sleep on the ground y'know.) We brought our Husky "Charlie" along for fun too. Once we arrived, we set up our tent and tried to beat the setting sun. As it got dark we made a small fire, and were just relaxing! We fell asleep in the tent watching the stars.

At about 2am, we were awakened by the sound of something moving thru the trees. Out in the country like that, you might hear something from 100 yards away but it sounded really close. Then about 10 minutes later, this time sounding about 50 yards away and getting closer, we heard more rustling thru the trees. Then we heard snorting sounds! Uhm.... "What is that?" I asked Kelley. Charlie looked at us both like we were crazy for being out there.

Then the rustling sounded closer. Whatever this was, it was

coming closer and closer to our tent.

"Ok." I thought to myself, "If this is a huge wild hog, we don't want to mess with him." My truck was right by the tent and I told Kelley if we heard it get any closer we were running into the truck!

Again, we heard some movement and more snorting It was definately closer. Kel is the more adventurous of the two of us. Obviously. I'm like a total art and music, take it easy kinda guy. She runs marathons and wants to be the first in line for any adventure. She grabbed the flashlight and shined it out through the tent. "I want to see this thing!" She said with excitement in her voice!

That was when we could see a pair of eyes looking back at us in the darkness, glowing in the light of the flashlight. This thing was big, whatever it was! It's eyes were about a foot apart from each other, this thing had a giant head!

The next thing we knew we could see not one, not two, but three sets of eyes all staring back at us. "Set off the alarm on your truck and see if they run off!" She screamed! I did, and nothing happened, they didn't even flinch.

"Into the truck now!" I shouted. Kelley and I ran out of the tent, jumped into the truck, and tossed Charlie in with us. "Turn on your headlights, I want to see them!" Kelley screamed. I started my truck and turned on the headlights.

That is when we saw them.

Right before our eyes, were three...... giant....... milk cows.

They were just laying there in the bushes looking at us like we were weird.

Back into the tent we went, laughing. Times like this make me think that I am, in fact, not a real man. Ahaaaaaa.... wow, cows.

# THANK YOU FOR THE SCARS

On another camping by myself I had a neat experience. I told my wife I was going to rough it. I took a tent, sleeping bag, inflatable mattress, computer, dvd's, several long extension chords, an igloo full of soda and hot pockets. I was hardly roughing it. I also took my piano keyboard out to the woods, along with a pair of headphones.

I'm sure it was a hilarious sight, as hikers would pass by and see a guy sitting under a tree next to a tent playing a piano with big headphones on his head. I will say it's pretty amazing to play the piano outdoors in the woods.

One morning while I was playing the piano, a thought popped into my mind, "What is the first thing that you would say to Jesus if you saw Him right now?" Without really thinking too much, the first thing that came to mind was, "Thank You for the scars." "Thank You for all You went through to be my sacrifice."

I continued to play, and then wrote a song with the same title. Just then a breeze came across the field and through the trees. I was reminded of the times in scripture when the Holy Spirit is referred to as a fresh wind.  It was a beautiful moment.  I pray that the song leads people into His presence.


lyrics:

*There, the wind is in my hair. I feel you everywhere,*
*but how i long to see you*

*One day, on that perfect someday, I will see you there,*
*and thank you for the scars*

*I'll say... Thank You,  Thank You lord*
*for the scars you bear for me,  for the cross that set me free*

*Thank You, Thank You Lord*
*even when my heart was very far*
*Thank you for the scars*


*Friday, dark and lonely friday. When you took my sin,*
*and shame upon your back*

*Sunday, on that perfect Sunday. When you showed the world,*
*what it means to love*

A week to remember

In late 2009, I experienced God's faithfulness, love and strength in an amazing and surreal way. It was all within the context of one crazy week. They are 7 days that I will remember for the rest of my life.

MONDAY- I woke up to see that I had several missed calls from my sweet mom I knew something must be up. After connecting to my voicemail, I heard her voice on the message saying that she had taken my dad to the emergency room.

After calling her back, I jumped in my truck and headed there. My dad had been having a lot of back pain over several months and finally came to a breaking point.

That day we found out that he had cancer and it had already progressed far, even into his bones.

I have amazing parents. I've been beyond blessed by the Lord to have a Mom and Dad that love me and have always supported me. They have both shown me what it means to keep your word, love unconditionally, and to have a strong work ethic. God first, family second, and everything else somewhere down the line. Even under this current pressure, I could see God's love at work in my family.

You need to know that my dad has an amazing sense of humor. Even that day in the emergency room, I could see that his heart was to somehow put the nurses at ease with humor. Even though he was the one laying on the hospital bed with an IV in his arm, he was cracking people up. As he was given a strong pain medication thru the IV in his arm it wasn't 5 seconds before he said, "Whoa... what did you give me?!?!" The nurse said "Nubain. This will help with the pain."

Dad asked, "NewBang?"

"Nubain." She replied.

"NewBang?????" He asked again, laughing.

"No, Nubain. N - U - B - A - I - N." politely spelling it out with a smile on her face.

He said, "If you give me that shot again, and this little side rail on my bed isn't up, I'll probably fall out of this bed, and there WILL BE a new bang."

She laughed, we all laughed, he wanted us to laugh. I saw the true character come out in my dad even in the crappiest of circumstances. He really has a heart for other people. Most of what he talked about that day was how this would effect my mom. She is always first on his list of concerns. Amazing.

TUESDAY- I got a call from a good friend about another tragedy. A well known evangelist and speaker who I had done ministry with had tragically taken his own life. He left a wife and beautiful children behind. He was 41.

WEDNESDAY- Shannon Becker, a radio promoter I had been working with, sent me a text saying several cities had added my song, "The Carpenter" to their play list. "Daytona, Las Vegas, Long Island and Chicago all added the song today." I received the text while in Brenham with my dad. Having a song on the radio seemed to mean nothing in comparison.
THURSDAY- I attended the funeral of my friend. The service was beautiful, and we were reminded that his legacy would not be how his life ended, but rather how his life was lived. It was

sad to see his family on the front row of the packed church.

FRIDAY- Snow fell in Houston. Amazing. It had been 5 years since this had occurred and even then, it was a light snow. On this day it was REALLY coming down, and it was beautiful. We made a snow man.

SATURDAY- I played and sang at a wedding for a young couple just starting off their new life together. I have known the bride since she was 11 years old.

SUNDAY- I stood in front of a church to lead worship while trying to fight back all the emotion of the week. I tried to hold off tears and a cracking voice. In in spite of how I felt, I acknowledged that God is still God, and that God is so incredibly good!

7 days.

7 days that I'll remember always. Within the ups and downs of life in those 7 days, I will say that God touched my heart. It was a week that had the highest highs and the lowest lows, all thrown in there together.

The only thing better than a snow day in Houston, is 2 snow days. I put my Siberian Husky, Charlie, on the leash and we walked down the street. We walked down the very center of the street with snow falling all around us. If you have ever been outside under falling snow, you know the sound I'm talking about. Yep, it's the lack of sound that you hear. Somehow all the falling snow created a kind of sound blanket over the area, and it was extremely quiet.

As I walked in the hush of snowfall, all bundled up, I took a deep breath. Before I could even begin to pray, it's almost as if God spoke first. What I heard in my heart was, "Do you see all these snowflakes, more than any human could count, falling all around you in every direction for as far as the eye can see? I have more love for your dad than the number of these. I have more grace for the family that experieced loss. For if you were to count all of the flakes, they would not begin to compare to my love."

I don't know about you, but I am so thankful that we are not left to walk through this life alone.

When David prayed in Psalm 23, he nailed it. "Even though I walk thru the valley of the shadow of death... I shall fear no evil, for thy rod and thy staff they comfort me. You anoint my head with oil, my cup overflows. Surely goodness and mercy will follow me all the days of my life, and I will dwell in the house of the Lord forever."

If you are having one of those weeks, turn to Him, and trust Him. If you are having one of those weeks where everything seems perfect, turn to Him, acknowledge and thank Him. I'm still in the learning process, but I am seeing over and over that God delights in having a true, intimate relationship with His created ones.

We have good weeks, and sometimes really tough ones.
God never ever changes.

ONE VOICE

18 CITIES.
8 STATES.
2 COUNTRIES.
1 VAN. 4600 MILES
10 AIRPLANES.
1 JESUS.

LIVE WORSHIP
WAYNE KERR

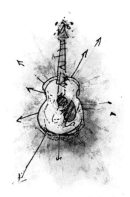

# ONE VOICE.

This book started with my deperate season of asking God what was next in my life as I retreated with Him in the mountains of New Mexico. He did speak to me on the mountain and I walked away knowing I was loved and that I still had a lot of work to do, music to make, songs to write. However, His specific plans weren't revealed to me until a few weeks later.

One Voice was God's idea. God woke me up in the middle of the night with His plan. I couldn't believe it. Basically I feel as if God said, "Go and lead worship. Go to any church or group that will have you, take your recording gear, and record the voices of my people in worship. Then take their voices and mix them all together so they will be singing with one another."

Different denominations, different cities and states, different age groups, but one Jesus. One Voice.

As I laid there in the dark at about 5am, I was wondering, "God is this you? Or did I eat too much mexican food late last night?" It was definately God.

I could see it all before me and it was pretty amazing. I felt as if God said "Go". Go for free... sing for free, and give the music away for free too. I thought I could give a free download card out to every single person who was at these events. Even the idea for the "tour shirt" was divine. This is the phrase that would appear on the back, "I sang on the OneVoice project, and got no royalties, but sang for Royalty."  I might think of myself as a semi-creative person, but this entire thing was really more than I could have dreamed up, it was truly a God thing.

After sending out some email feelers, word started spreading, and several cites started saying, "We'll host a One Voice concert!" Three concerts turned into five. Five turned into ten, and so on. The next thing I knew, I was about to set off on a 17 city, 8 state, 4500 mile driving, multiple plane flying, cross country international journey.

One of the things that started to amaze me was how clearly God was making clear His bigger plan... that ALL people would worship Him together. Before I knew it, I could see how the tour would include Methodist churches, Baptist churches, Non-Denominational churches, Lutheran churches, Catholic churches and more! As I looked at the calendar, I stood amazed.

I was also believing that the nations would be somehow represented on this recording. How that would happen, I wasn't really sure, but I knew this was to be more than an "American" project. The nations should be represented on this CD. I was taking a class called Perspectives, and I was reminded of every tribe and nation worshipping before the throne of Jesus. Getting the nations represented was a huge step of faith. God would have to make this happen.

2 years ago, I was booked to play in Japan and Singapore. Kelley and I were completely blown away and showered in love by all of the amazing folks in Singapore. I somehow knew in my heart that Singapore was to be represented on this CD! Crazy, I know. On top of that, I felt as if my entire band would go as well. I even put Singapore on the tour shirt by faith, because I felt God's leading was so clear.

As I was about to venture out on the first dates of the OneVoice driving tour, my friend, Bernice, from Singapore dropped me a note online. "Hey Wayne, when are you coming back to Singapore?" Ahaaaaa, I laughed as I typed a reply into my laptop. "I was just about to contact you guys!" I explained what God was up to in my heart, and told her that I truly believed Singapore was to be represented on the recording. In what capacity, how or when, I had no earthly idea.

Her response came back, "Let's pray about it! I've told our pastor and youth pastor about the idea and we'll see what God is up to!"

I launched out on the tour. Dallas, Tx., Sacramento, Ca., Portland, Or., and Lake Charles, La. Following those dates would be my solo driving tour that would go thru 6 states. This would all happen in my amazing tour bus... oh wait, just kidding, I would go in a white Toyota mini-van rental. I travel in style.

At about this same time, I'd heard back from Singapore. They said they were believing to put 2-3 churches together and host an event. They had looked into flights, and they were quite expensive. $1500 a person.

I was so excited to see the email. She was probably shocked to see my response, "I would love to see if we could get the entire band over there! We would all play for free, if we could somehow get the travel covered." I was basically believing for at least $6000 to come across my lap to get us there. I say dream big, we serve a big God!

Midland, Tx., Carlsbad, Nm., Durango, Co., Texarkana, Tx.,

Broken Arrow, Ok., then into Missouri: Stockton, Eagle Rock, Chillicothe, and Albany. So many great people. It was such a joy and true blessing to connect with Gods people. On the coasts, in the heartland, in the mountains, in big cities, and in small towns. I experienced God's creation and His people. Amazing.

At this point, I was already over half way done with the tour. Singapore responded and said they would officially be glad to host a OneVoice event. I remember Bernice saying, "Let's keep praying."

Something was going on... I didn't fully, and don't fully understand. But what I do know is this: God is worthy of our worship. When I say "our" I'm talking humanity. I'm talking ALL peoples, ALL nations, ALL languages!

I got a phone call from my sweet amazing bride. She seemed suuuuper excited. "What's up?" I asked.

"Ok, are you sitting down?" she asked.

"Uhm, yes, I'm driving. Should I pull over?" I responded.

"I just want to make sure you are sitting down!"

She said, "What is one of the main things you are believing for on this OneVoice Tour?"

"Uhhhmmmm, that people will actually come to these concerts?" I said.

"No!!! The MAIN thing?!?" She said louder.

"Uhhhhhhhmmmmmmmm... that this mini-van will survive this 4500 mile trip I'm on?"

"NOOOoooo..." now laughing, "What's the MAIN THING?" She asked again even louder this time!

"To get to go with my band to Singapore?" I said.

"YES!!!" She went on to explain, that on that very day while on a mission trip in Galveston, something amazing and God sized had happened. She was fixing a house with a few families from our church. One of the amazing families asked... "What is Wayne up to these days?" She explained that I was on this crazy adventure, doing 17 shows for free, believing God to work the money part out, recording all these voices together for a CD called OneVoice. She then shared how I was even believing to get the finances together so the entire band could get to Singapore to include them on the project.

Then with no hesitation, he said, "Tell Wayne that whatever they do not come up with, my family and I would like to sponsor them to be able to make this happen."

Wow.

At this point, I pulled over in disbelief. God had made a way. I couldn't believe it, yet I fully believed it, all at the same time. This was all His idea in the first place, and sure enough, God provided! I stand in amazement even now. When God says, "Go," just go... He created the universe, your DNA, all the stars and time itself. I think you can trust Him.

This family will remain nameless. But to them I say, thank you for investing in His ministry. Thank you for being such cheerful and generous givers! I pray God blesses your family 100 fold, not only financially, but with peace, joy, healing and even more hope in your household.

Are you listening to God today?

He has great plans for you and He will provide!

While I was up on that mountain I spent much of the time praying. Before I started asking God, "What's next for me?," and all those kinds of questions, I began to just say "Thank You."

Thank You God for an amazing incredible summer, Thank You for 11 straight weeks of camp. I fully understand that all 11 of those ministries could have been asking me for the same week on the calendar. I trust that Gods hand had provided my all those opportunities.

Thank You God for my incredible wife and best friend, Kelley. Why God would you bless me with such an amazing girl to walk through this life with? A girl who has an overflowing heart of ministry that pours out on whoever she meets. Thank You.

Thank You God for my family. Why God would you bless me with the most fantastic parents, Roger and JoAnn Kerr? Parents who both told me from a young age that I could do whatever I wanted to do with my life... and then not only said those words, but backed it up in deed, backed it up in love. Thank You.

Thank You God for amazing friends and partners in ministry...

Why God would you put guys like Matt Kidd into my life, who is so talented, so humble, and is such a great friend. Why God would you put guys in my life like Raymond Turner, Joel and Jonathan Camey, Josh Anderson, Randy Harvey, Rodney Black, Abel Orta Jr., Nolan Burke, Razmandi... and tons more. Guys who would be TRUE friends, some of which not only stood in my wedding, but would love me enough to be honest with me! Thank You.

The "Thank You" list continued on and on.

I suggest you jot down what you are thankful for today...

Go ahead...

Put this book down, and grab a pen.

It'll only take a few minutes, and trust me... your soul will be uplifted, and God will turn His ear towards a thankful heart. So many times, I flat out do not take the time to be thankful.

(I'll wait here- see you in a few minutes)

(I've even given you some space here to write on)

_____

_____

_____

_____

_____

_____

_____

Welcome back. I don't know about you, but for me, something pretty amazing happens when we come before Almighty God, and simply say "Thank You."

After my time of saying thanks to God, I moved into the "What am I doing with my life GOD?!?!?!!?" section. I truthfully and honestly just came before God and shared my worries, shared my fears, just like talking to my best friend. Then I said, "God, whatever you have next for me is what I want to do." Then I prayed, "Lord, I want to be who you want me to be, and not focus so much on "What" I'm doing."

Did you notice a shift in my prayer? Even as I began praying, I felt God's heart being less concerned with "what I do", and more concerned with "who I am." I too slowly began to feel less worried about my next musical venture, and felt God gently remind me that He is more after my heart condition.

How am I walking out my faith? In my home... in my marriage... with my friends... with strangers.

# CONCLUSION

So here I sit typing this final chapter. Most of the OneVoice Tour has wrapped up. One week from today, my band and I will board a plane bound for Asia, connecting from San Francisco to Hong Kong, then onto Singapore. Amazing. This tour will end as it began, in worship of the Almighty. The One who wakes His people from their sleep and gives them dreams. The One who prepares the way and provides all that would ever be needed. I think it's fitting that I am now about to wrap up this book while still in the midst of the amazing journey.

Thank you so much for taking the time to allow me to share these adventures with you. I pray you have been encouraged in some small way through these pages.

God is alive and well and at work in the lives of people today, just as He has always been. I hope you hear this today... God doesn't only work through Christian musicians, pastors or speakers. God uses students, executives, moms, dads and families who are willing!

"The eyes of the Lord search the whole earth in order to strengthen those whose hearts are fully committed to Him." 2 Chronicles 16:9

I am no one special, just a guy who marvels at the goodness and grace of the Almighty. At the end of the day, I'm still learning that the whole thing has been designed this way. God desires to do exactly what He has done all through scripture... make His NAME known all over the world, to all nations. Gen 12:3
He wants to use you and me to do that, crazy as it sounds. And I believe, the thing that delights His heart so much, is when we get to experience walking through this life with Him. God has plans for you!

If you have never given the "steering wheel" of your life to Christ, please do it now... Just pray from the bottom of your heart and ask Jesus to rule and reign in your life. Then buckle up my friend. The ride is more amazing than you would have ever dreamed.

His blessings to you.

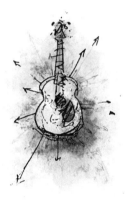

for more information on wayne's ministry
please visit

**www.waynekerrmusic.com**